CHALLENGE

LONGMAN GEOGRAPHY

Authors:

Jane Bramwell   Clare Brooks   Andy Buck   John Pallister   Claire Rohdie

Series editor: Vincent Bunce

LONGMAN

Addison Wesley Longman Limited
Edinburgh Gate, Harlow, Essex, CM20 2JE

© Addison Wesley Longman 1996

All rights reserved. No part of this publication may be reproduced, stored in a retrieval system, or transmitted in any form or by any means, electronic, mechanical, photocopying, recording, or otherwise, without either the prior written permission of the Publishers or a licence permitting restricted copying issued by the Copyright Agency Ltd, 90 Tottenham Court Road, London W1P 9HE

First published 1996

ISBN 0582 27547 4

Set in Zaps Elliptical 11/14pt

Printed in Great Britain by Scotprint Limited, Musselburgh, Scotland.

The Publishers' policy is to use paper manufactured from sustainable forests.

Design and production by The Wooden Ark Studio
Illustrations by Phill Burrows, Joan Corlass, Tony Richardson, David Cook,
Picture research by Louise Edgeworth
Cover design by Ship
Cover illustration by John Clementson

We are grateful to the following teacher's for their valuable contribution to the manuscripts in this series:

Scotland
Susan Telfer, Linlithgow Academy, Stirlingshire

England and Wales
Tony Dodsworth, Pope Pius X RC Comprehensive School, South Yorkshire
Marion Dungworth, Swinton Comprehensive School, South Yorkshire
Ian Milford, Stoke Damerel Community College, Devon
Kirsten Reynolds, Fakenham High School, Norwich
Kevin Williams, Notley High School, Essex

Acknowledgements

We are grateful to the following for permission to reproduce photographs and other copyright material:

Ace Photo Agency, page 70(John Delaney); Air Namibia, page 87; Andy Buck, pages 80, 82 left, 83, 88. Vincent Bunce, pages 21 centre, 42, 84; J .Allan Cash, pages 21 above, 22, 32 below, 50, 54; c Crown Copyright, pages 9 left, 11, 32-33; Robert Harding Picture Library, pages 4 below, 69(Tony Gervis), 78 left(Israel Talby); The Image Bank, page 24(Kaz Mori); Images Colour Library, page 21 below; Images of India, page 76(James Mitchell); Landform Slides, page 25; Link, pages 82 left(Les Bush), 86 above(Rogan Coles); Marco Polo, page 56(M.Blanchard); NHPA, pages 36 above & 44(Anthony Bannister); Network, pages 61(Nikolai Ignatiev), 71(Michael Abrahams); J.Pallister, pages 4 above, 5, 6, 9 right, 10, 13, 16, 39, 42, 43, 47; Ross Parry Picture Agency, page 20 below; Planet Earth Pictures, page 36 below; Popperfoto, page 78-79(Reuter); Claire Rohdiè, page 86 bottom; Science Photo Library, page 15(Earth Satellite Corporation); Tony Stone Images, pages 20 above & 32 above(Shaun Egan), 31(Barry Marsden), 64, 65 above(Jon Riley), 74(Mark Segal); TRIP, page 65 below(B.Turner); WaterAid, page 58(Caroline Penn).

Contents

Rivers and floods — 4

1
- The benefits of rivers — 5
- The water cycle — 6
- The river in the hills — 8
- The river in the lowlands — 10
- Why do rivers flood? — 12
- The mighty Mississippi — 14
- Responding to floods — 16
- River journey — 18

Coasts — 20

2
- Using the coast — 21
- Waves — 22
- Eroding the coast — 24
- Change along the coast — 26
- Building up the land — 28
- Coastal hazards — 30
- Focus on the Dorset coast — 32
- Coastal development — 34

Ecosystems — 36

3
- Why are plants important? — 37
- Natural Ecosystems — 38
- How does climate affect vegetation — 40
- Using ecosystems — 42
- The savanna ecosystem — 44
- The changing savanna — 46
- The challenge of preservation and conservation — 48

Managing environments — 50

4
- National Parks — 51
- The changing British countryside — 52
- The Norfolk Broads — 54
- Managing Alpine environments — 56
- Water management — 58
- Oil in the tundra — 60
- Last resort for the Mediterranean? — 62

Population — 64

5
- The challenge of population growth — 65
- Population growth — 66
- How are we spread out? — 68
- Why do people move? — 70
- Is there a population challenge? — 72
- Resources and population — 74
- Managing population change — 76
- Rising to the challenge — 78

Sustainable development — 80

6
- Developing Namibia — 81
- Water in Namibia — 82
- Water for Windhoek — 84
- Fishing for success — 86
- Small scale sustainable development — 88
- The green plan — 90
- Issues in geography — 92

Glossary — 94

Index — 96

Rivers and floods

Rivers are a valuable natural resource. People depend on them for many things. In this unit you will find out about:

- the main features of rivers and valleys
- why rivers sometimes flood
- how people try to control river behaviour.

Source 1

Flood damage from a river

- What flood damage can you see in Source 1?
- Why do people live in an area such as this?
- Would the people living here still think that the advantages of living close to the river outweighed the risks?

Rivers and floods

The benefits of rivers

How far is your home or school from the nearest river or stream? For many of you the answer will be 'within easy walking distance'. This is because the original site for many settlements was next to a river. A local water supply was vital in the days before water came out of taps.

As well as offering low and sheltered land on the valley floor, a riverside location has other advantages such as:

- transport
- defence
- food supply.

When you live around 1,600 kilometres from the sea in the middle of Brazil, it is the river's sand banks that you use as the 'beach' (Source 2).

Source 2
Sunday afternoon on the banks of the River Negro, Brazil.

Source 3
The benefits of rivers

Activity 1

With the help of Source 3, outline the benefits of rivers using the following headings:
- **Water supply**
- **Leisure and recreation**
- **Transport**
- **Energy**

Activity 2

Look at Source 4.

a) Write down the percentages for water use in the home.

b) Show the percentages on a pie chart.

c) Design a poster to show how people could cut down on their use of water in the home.

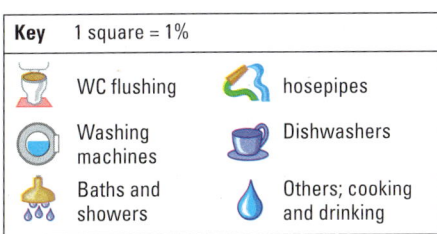

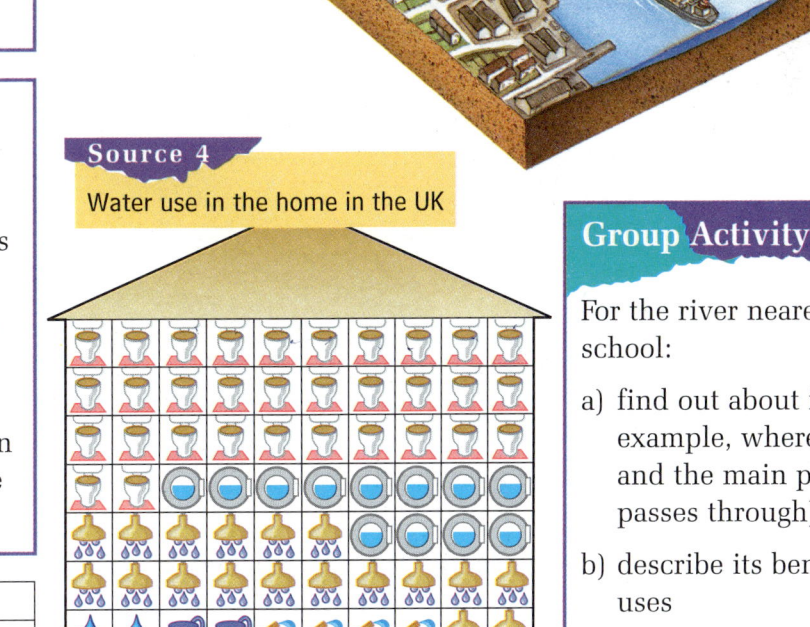

Source 4
Water use in the home in the UK

Key 1 square = 1%
- WC flushing
- Washing machines
- Baths and showers
- hosepipes
- Dishwashers
- Others; cooking and drinking

Group Activity

For the river nearest to school:

a) find out about it (for example, where it begins and the main places it passes through)

b) describe its benefits and uses

c) draw a map or make sketches to show how the river and the land around it are used.

The water cycle

There's an awful lot of water in the world: but most of it is salt water not fresh water. Only 13 per cent of the world's water is fresh water (Source 1). More than half of that is locked up in the ice of Antarctica which is well away from where most people live (Source 2). Energy from the sun evaporates the water from the seas and oceans. In the atmosphere the water vapour cools and condenses to give **precipitation**. A lot of the rain that falls makes its way into rivers. Rivers return the water to the seas and oceans. This is the water cycle (Source 3).

Source 2
Antarctica: a great store of fresh water

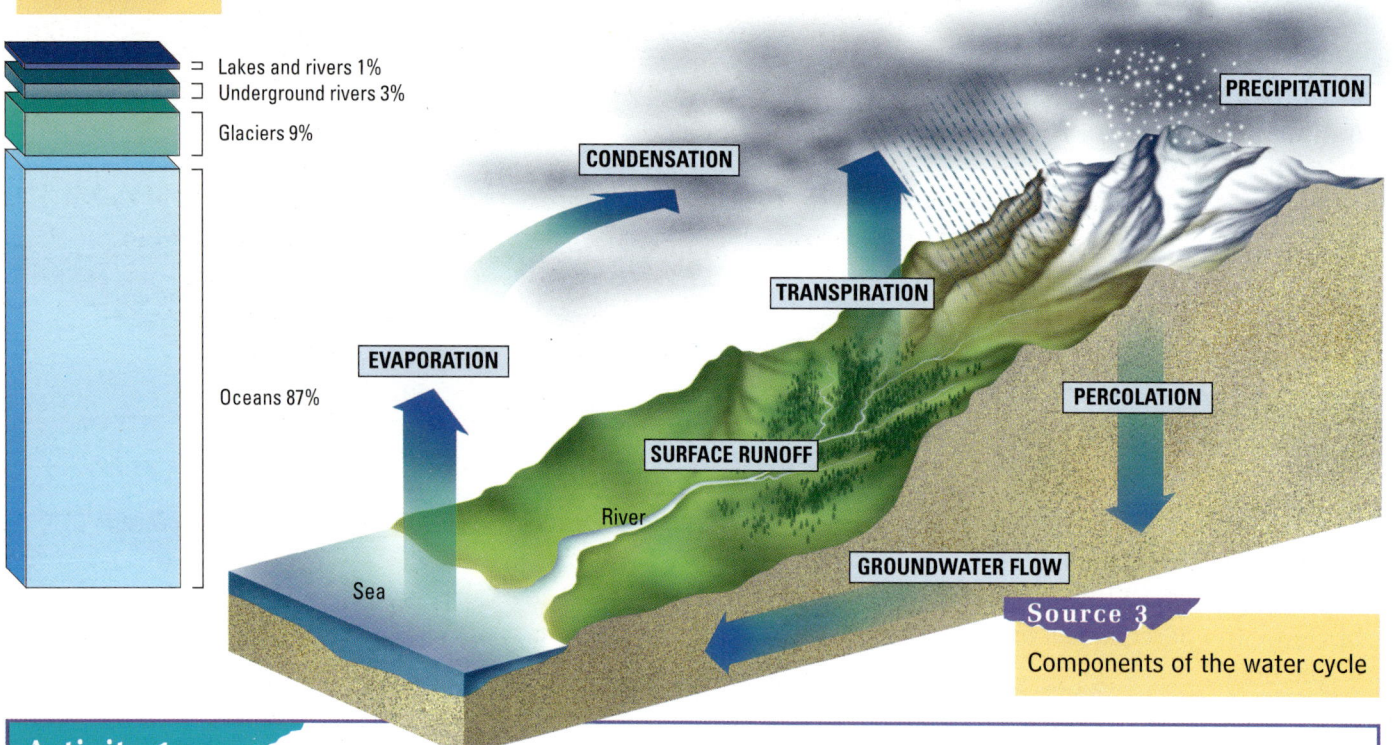

Source 1
Water stores

- Lakes and rivers 1%
- Underground rivers 3%
- Glaciers 9%
- Oceans 87%

Source 3
Components of the water cycle

Labels: CONDENSATION, PRECIPITATION, TRANSPIRATION, EVAPORATION, PERCOLATION, SURFACE RUNOFF, GROUNDWATER FLOW, River, Sea

Activity 1

Write out the following sentences. Use the terms in the boxes on Source 3 to fill in the gaps.

By the process of _____ water from the earth's surface is changed into water vapour in the atmosphere. Cooling of the water vapour leads to the process of _____ which forms clouds. Clouds may grow tall enough for rain or snow to fall, which are examples of _____ . Of the rain which falls, some of the water goes into rivers as _____; some is intercepted by trees and returned to the atmosphere by the process of _____; some sinks downwards into the ground called _____ . The groundwater may reach rivers or seas by _____ .

Rivers and floods

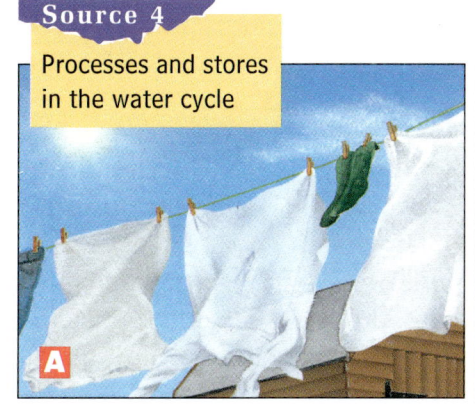

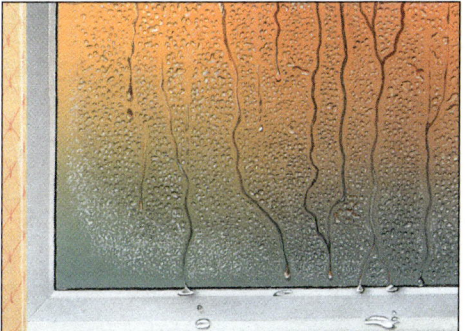

Source 4
Processes and stores in the water cycle

A — Processes

B — Stores

Do you understand the term 'store'? At certain points in the cycle, water movement is checked. Think of a store as being like a sponge. It soaks up the water and holds it for a time as it travels through the system.

Rivers are a vital part of the earth's water cycle. Rivers transfer rain water across the land to sea. Sometimes not much of the rain which falls reaches the river. For example, the rain may be light, the slopes gentle, the rock porous and there may be trees to intercept the rain.

Activity 2

a) Describe in your own words what is happening in each sketch in Source 4A.

b) Give the term from the boxes in Source 3 which fits each sketch.

c) Name the stores marked X, Y and Z in Source 4B.

d) Explain some of the reasons why such stores are important to people.

e) When store Y is low, how do you think people are affected?

Activity 3

Make a large copy of Source 5. Add labels to explain why not much of the rain that falls will run off over the surface into the river.

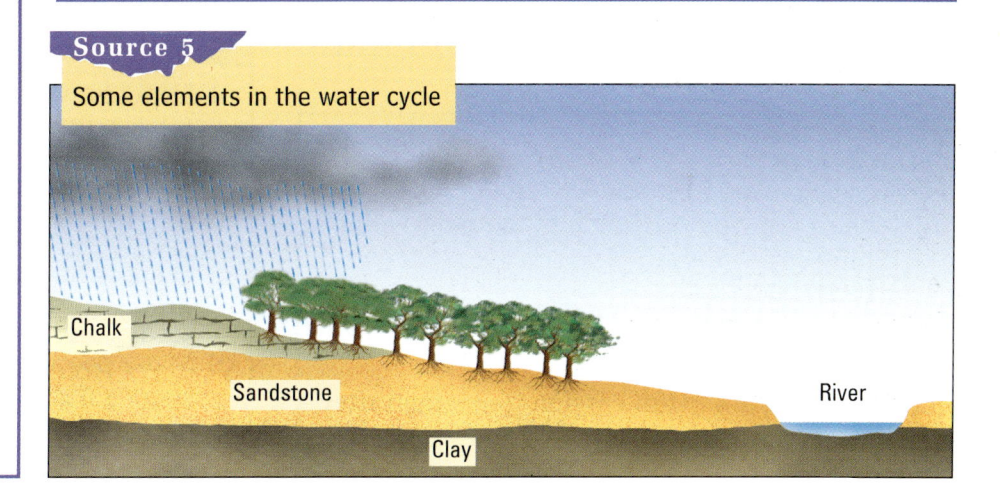

Source 5
Some elements in the water cycle

Chalk, Sandstone, Clay, River

The river in the hills

Near its source in the hills the river is quite small. The water is shallow and the bed of the **channel** is full of stones. You may have crossed such a river using the stones as stepping stones. The river bends from side to side at the bottom of a steep-sided V-shaped valley (Source 1). Where the edges of the higher ground force the river to bend around them, **interlocking spurs** are formed. The river is cutting into the rocks of the land by **vertical erosion**. It is called vertical because the river is cutting downwards. Erosion means the wearing away of rock. The main process of erosion by which the river does this is **abrasion**. This is when boulders bounced along the river bed break off pieces of rock as they are moved.

The river appears to flow fastest of all when it goes over **waterfalls**. These form where hard bands of rock outcrop. Hard rocks are more difficult for the river to erode (Source 2).

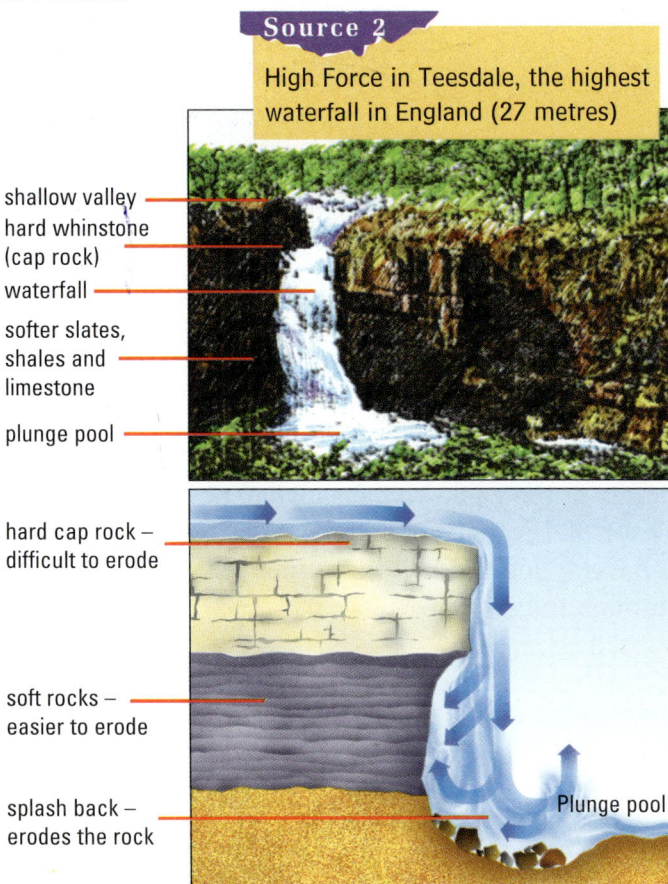

Source 1
The river valley in the hills

Labels: vertical erosion, V-shaped valley, interlocking spurs, steep sides

Source 2
High Force in Teesdale, the highest waterfall in England (27 metres)

Labels: shallow valley, hard whinstone (cap rock), waterfall, softer slates, shales and limestone, plunge pool

Cross-section labels: hard cap rock – difficult to erode, soft rocks – easier to erode, splash back – erodes the rock, Plunge pool

Activity 1

a) Make a copy of the sketch of the river valley (Source 1).

b) Add extra labels to your sketch for the features of the river and its channel.

c) Explain how vertical erosion forms the valley features shown.

Activity 2

a) Using Source 2, give three pieces of information about High Force.

b) Draw the cross-section of High Force and add to it the names of the rock types.

c) What is the plunge pool? How do you think it will form?

d) Many people visit High Force in Teeside. Write a leaflet (with pictures) which could be useful to them.

Rivers and floods

Source 3
OS map of part of Upper Teesdale

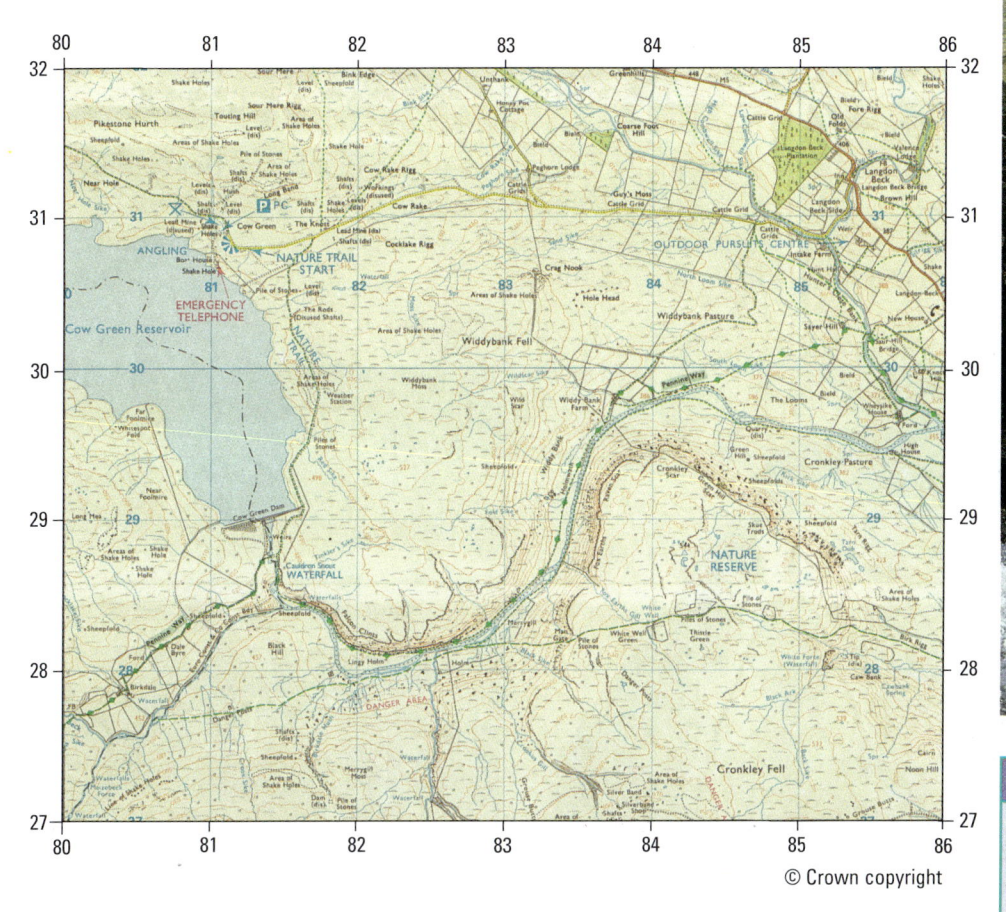

© Crown copyright

Source 4
Cauldron Snout

River processes

Abrasion: boulders are used to break off pieces of rock in the river.

Deposition: river drops sediment.

Erosion: river wears away the rock.

Lateral erosion: land worn away at the sides of the river.

Vertical erosion: land worn away by the river cutting down.

Activity 3

Use Source 3 for this activity.

a) Explain how the OS map shows that:
   i) the land is high   ii) the land is steep
   iii) not many people live here.

b) Put a heading 'Who uses Upper Teesdale?' Make a larger copy of the table below and complete it with the map evidence:

User	Purpose	Map evidence	Four figure grid reference
Water Board	water supply		
Visitors	leisure & tourism		
Farmers	sheep farming		
Army	shooting ranges		

c) The photograph (Source 4) was taken at 814287 looking south. What extra information does it give about Cauldron Snout and the land around it?

Group Activity

Find out about the Pennine Way or one of the other long-distance footpaths (if there is one closer to where you live). Draw a sketch map to show where it goes. Label and draw sketches of the features along the route.

The river in the lowlands

By the time it reaches its mouth the river is at its largest. The water is deep and the channel is wide. The channel bed is most likely to have a covering of sand-sized particles. The bends in the river have increased in size so much that they have formed **meanders**. Along the edges of the channel are raised banks called **levées**. Behind these is a wide area of flat land called the **floodplain**. It is here that **lateral erosion** takes place. This means that the river is wearing away the land at the side of the channel and on the sides of the valley. **Deposition** is now an important process as the river drops much of the load of sediment it was transporting (Sources 1 and 2).

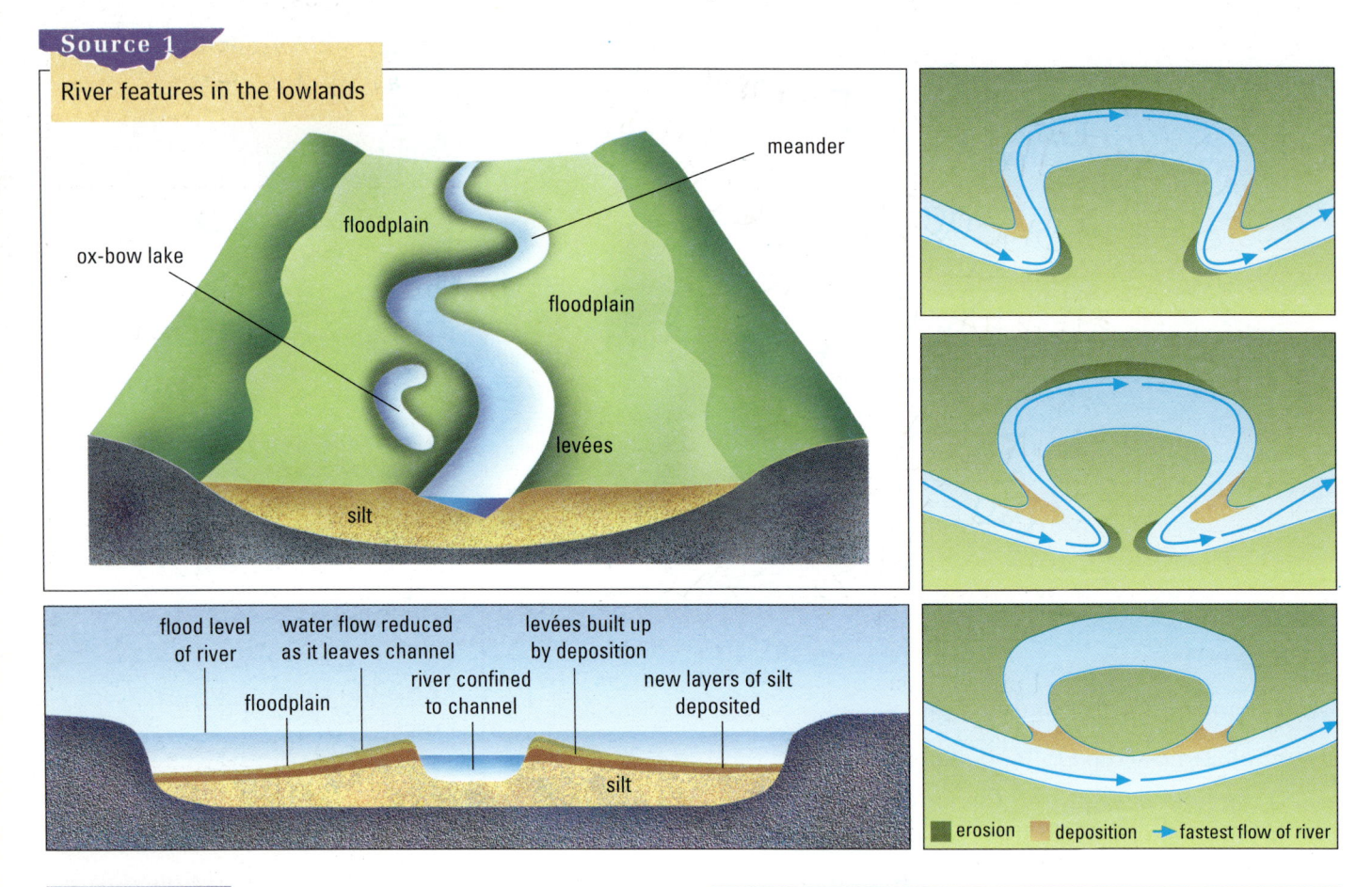

Source 1

River features in the lowlands

Source 2

Levées and floodplain of the River Mersey near Manchester

Activity 1

a) Make your own glossary box to describe the following features:

floodplain   levée   meander

b) With the help of diagrams, explain how a river which meanders can form an ox-bow lake.

c) Explain how flooding helps to form levées, floodplains and ox-bow lakes.

Rivers and floods

Source 3
OS map of the mouth of the River Tees

© Crown copyright

Source 4 shows the full drainage basin of the River Tees. It also gives some information about rainfall and river-flow levels in parts of the basin.

Activity 2

a) Explain how the OS map in Source 3 shows that:
  i) the land is low
  ii) the land is flat
  iii) many industries are located here
  iv) this part of the River Tees is used by ships.

b) Suggest reasons why the land next to the mouth of the Tees is a good location for industries.

Activity 3

Give the information from Source 4 which supports each of the following statements:

a) The River Tees has its source in the hills where the rainfall is high.

b) The amount of water flowing in the river increases from source to mouth.

Source 4
The drainage basin of the River Tees

Key:
- Land over 600m
- Land over 300m
- Land under 300m
- Edge of drainage basin
- Mean river flow m/sec
- Mean annual precipitation

Rainfall values: 1823mm, 1350mm, 570mm
Mean river flow values: 2.67, 13.50, 18.20

Locations: PENNINES, Cow Green Reservoir, Middleton, Barnard Castle, Darlington, Yarm, Stockton, Billingham, Middlesbrough, Hartlepool, CLEVELAND HILLS

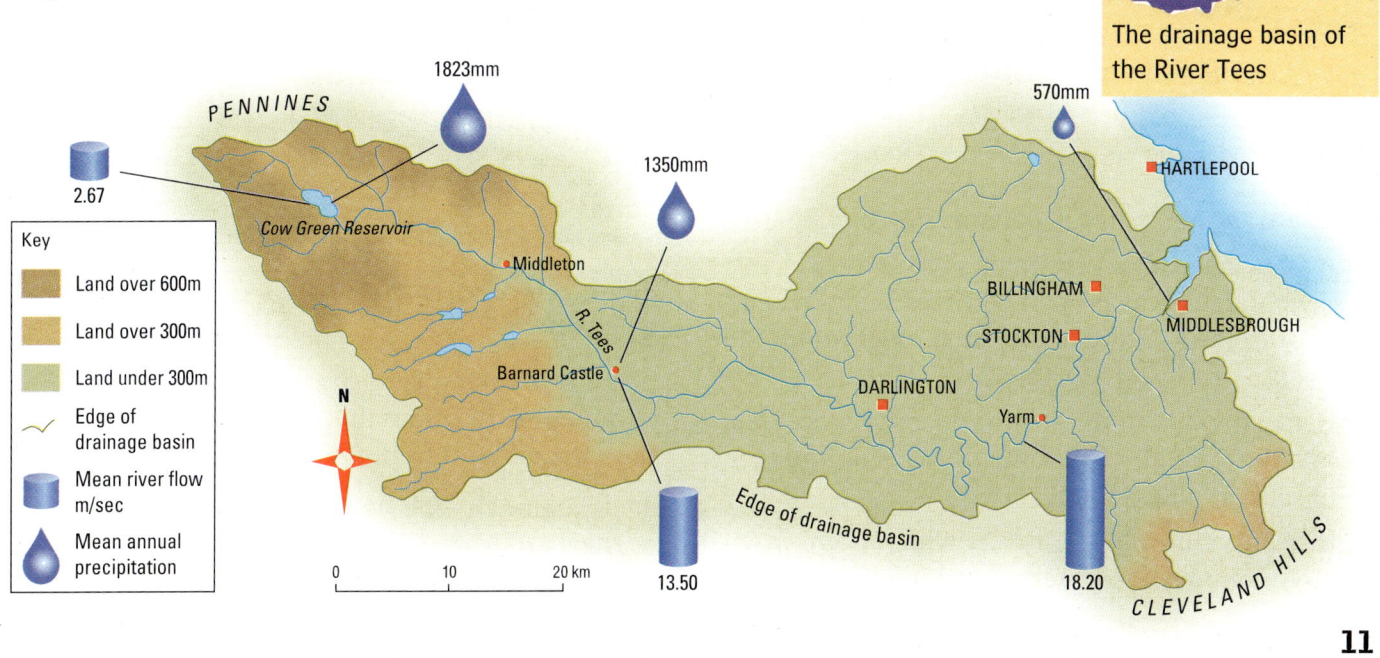

11

Why do rivers flood?

Rivers flood from natural causes. It is also natural for a river to flood a few times each year.

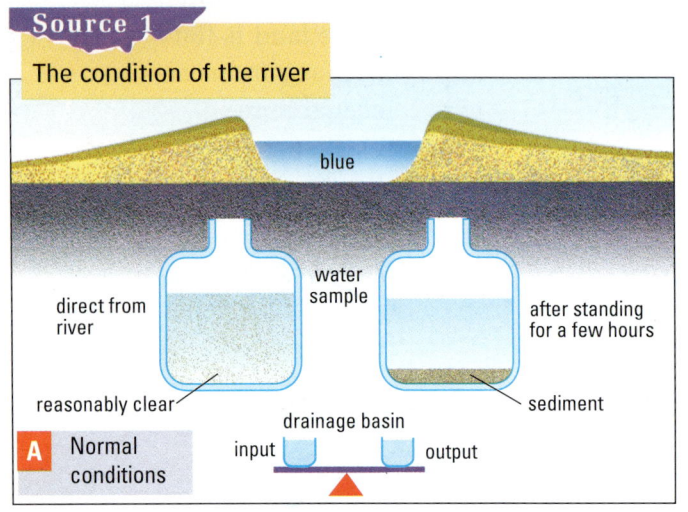

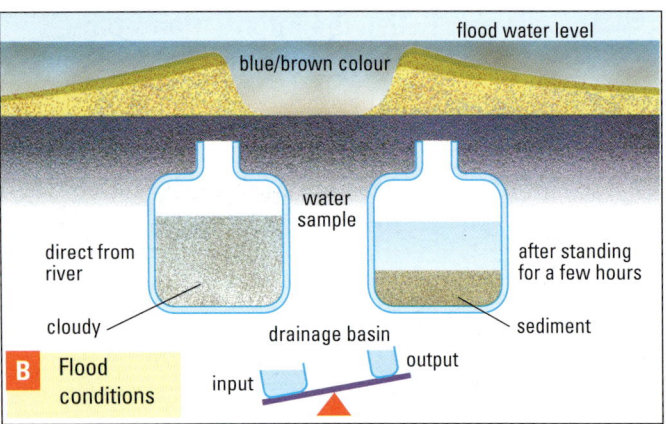

Source 1: The condition of the river

A Normal conditions
- blue
- direct from river: reasonably clear
- water sample
- after standing for a few hours: sediment
- drainage basin: input = output

B Flood conditions
- flood water level
- blue/brown colour
- direct from river: cloudy
- water sample
- after standing for a few hours: sediment
- drainage basin: input > output

Source 2: Why rivers flood

A Weather for the last seven days

Monday	total 25 mm
Tuesday	total 8 mm
Wednesday	total 15 mm
Thursday	total 13 mm
Friday	total 21 mm
Saturday	total 8 mm
Sunday	total 22 mm
Total	**112 mm**

B Rainfall during the storm

Time	Rainfall
8 – 9 am	13 mm
9 – 10 am	20 mm
10 – 11 am	22 mm
11 – noon	17 mm
noon – 1 pm	8 mm
1 pm – 2 pm	4 mm
Total	**84 mm**

C snowline in August, snowline in April, Glacier, edge of glacier in August, edge of glacier in April, River

Activity 1

Describe the ways in which a river is different when it is in flood (Source 1).

Source 2 shows the three natural causes of flooding:

1. A large amount of precipitation over a period of several days. The ground becomes saturated and most of the rain water goes as **surface runoff** into rivers.
2. Heavy precipitation. In a thunderstorm the rain hits the ground so hard that there is no time for it to soak into the ground.
3. Melting snow and ice. Rivers which begin in high mountain regions usually flood in summer.

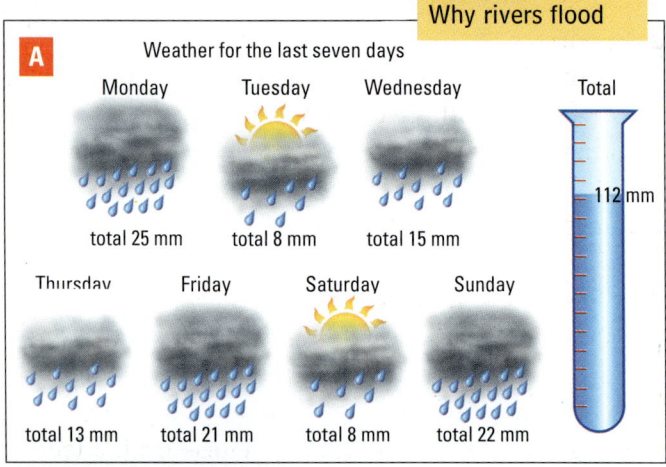

Activity 2

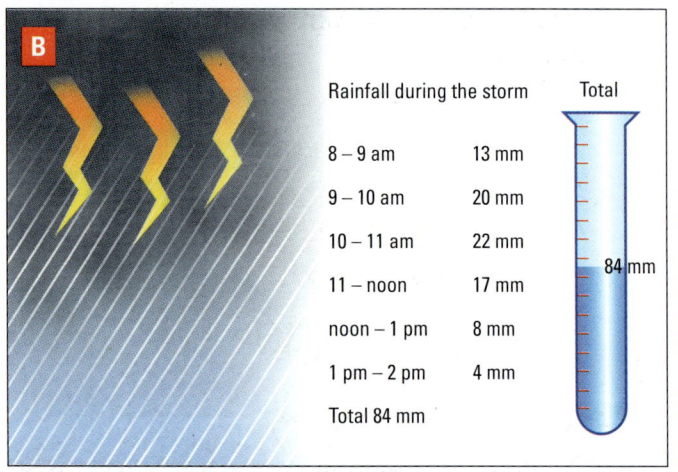

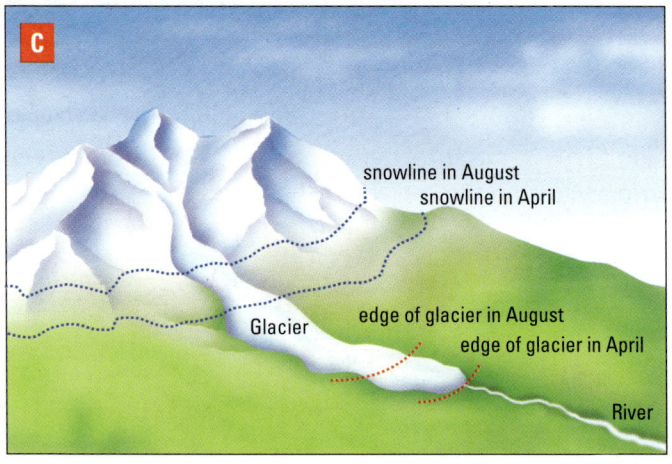

a) Draw bar graphs to show the daily rainfall amounts in A and the hourly rainfall amounts in B from Source 2.

b) Explain why these rainfall conditions are likely to lead to river flooding.

Rivers and floods

Some of the other natural features of the drainage basin, such as steep slopes, lack of vegetation and **impermeable rocks**, help to speed up **surface runoff**. This increases the chance of river flooding. People can also increase the chances of river floods occurring by altering how the land is used. Land use affects surface runoff. In urban areas, concrete and tarmac surfaces mean that water cannot seep into the ground. On buildings, water is caught in gutters and led rapidly into underground drains (Source 3). These drains feed water into the rivers. So rain water reaches rivers much more quickly than if it had landed on a vegetation-covered surface.

Source 3
Water movements in an urban environment

Rainfall → hits roof of house → into gutters → down drainpipe → into underground drain → underground pipe to river

Source 4
A summer thunderstorm in the USA

Source 5
Glacier in Argentina

You could say that it is people's own fault that they have problems with river floods. People should never have started to live in the flood zone next to rivers. The flat land beside a river is not called the floodplain without a good reason! However, the flat land with its covering of fertile silt was just too attractive for farming and settlement. People couldn't resist settling there. Also they believed that they could stop the river from flooding.

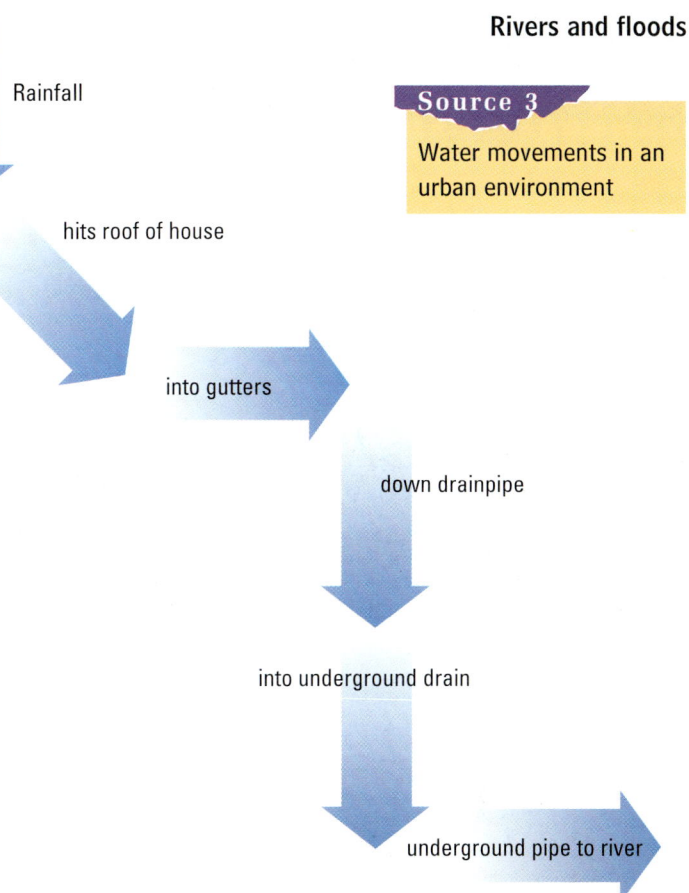

Activity 3

Look at Sources 4 and 5. Explain how natural and human features increase the chances of river flooding.

The mighty Mississippi

Despite being nicknamed 'Old Man River', the Mississippi and its tributaries are a 'mighty big' river system. There is, of course, no river to match the Amazon's size, but the Mississippi and its tributaries are among the top five rivers in the world (Source 1).

Source 1
The major rivers of the world

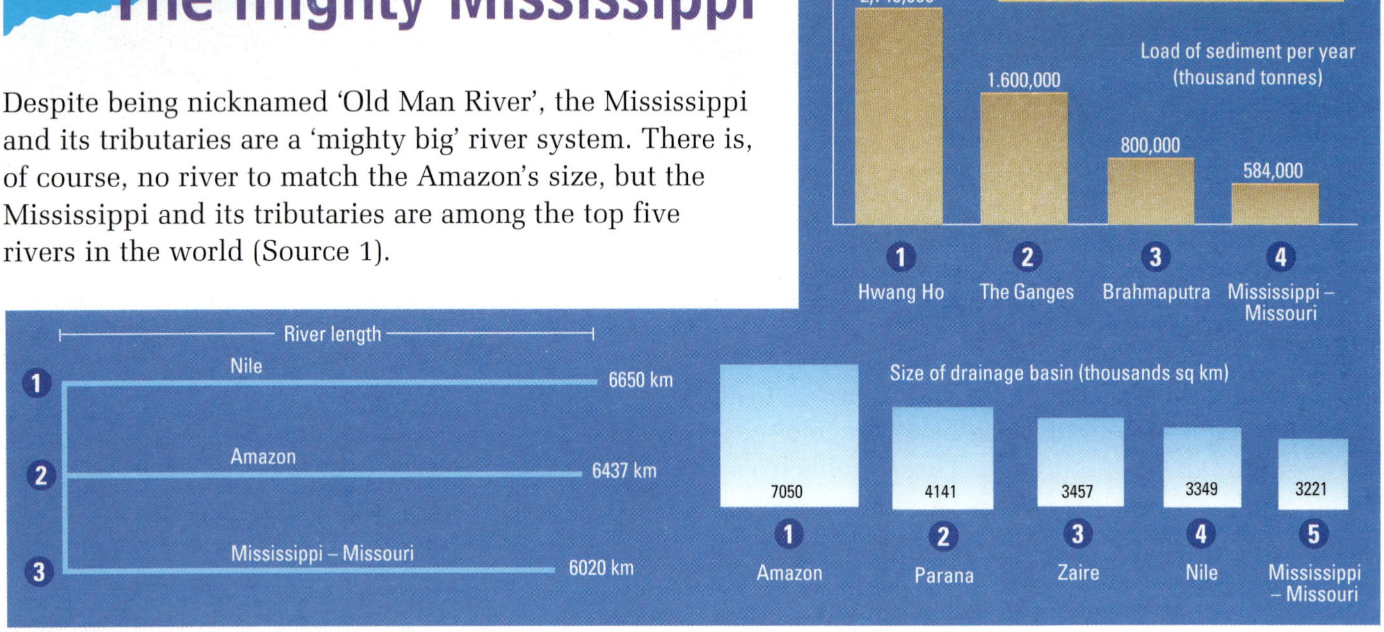

Load of sediment per year (thousand tonnes)
1. Hwang Ho — 2,740,000
2. The Ganges — 1,600,000
3. Brahmaputra — 800,000
4. Mississippi – Missouri — 584,000

River length
1. Nile — 6650 km
2. Amazon — 6437 km
3. Mississippi – Missouri — 6020 km

Size of drainage basin (thousands sq km)
1. Amazon — 7050
2. Parana — 4141
3. Zaire — 3457
4. Nile — 3349
5. Mississippi – Missouri — 3221

Source 2
The drainage basin of the Mississippi

Activity 1

Use an atlas. Show on an outline world map the courses of the big rivers named in Source 1.

You can also say that it is a 'mighty important river'. Rain water from over one-third of the USA drains into it and its tributaries (Source 2). It can be used by ships as far inland as Minneapolis. The farms in the Corn Belt have been described as 'the richest farms on earth'. Corn (or maize as we call it) is fed to animals (Source 3), and the food produced goes to all America's big cities.

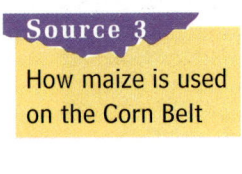

Source 3
How maize is used on the Corn Belt

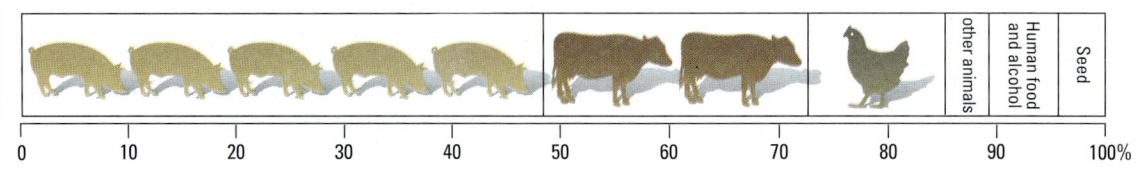

(bar chart showing: pigs ~0–50%, cows ~50–70%, chicken ~70–80%, other animals, Human food and alcohol, Seed up to 100%)

However, there is a problem: the Mississippi keeps on flooding. The Americans have been trying to cure this problem for the last one hundred years, but in 1993 the floods were the biggest ever seen (Source 4).

Activity 2

a) Describe what is mighty about the Mississippi River.

b) Why are the lowlands around the Mississippi so important for American food supplies?

Source 4

The Mississippi floods of 1993

Flooded area

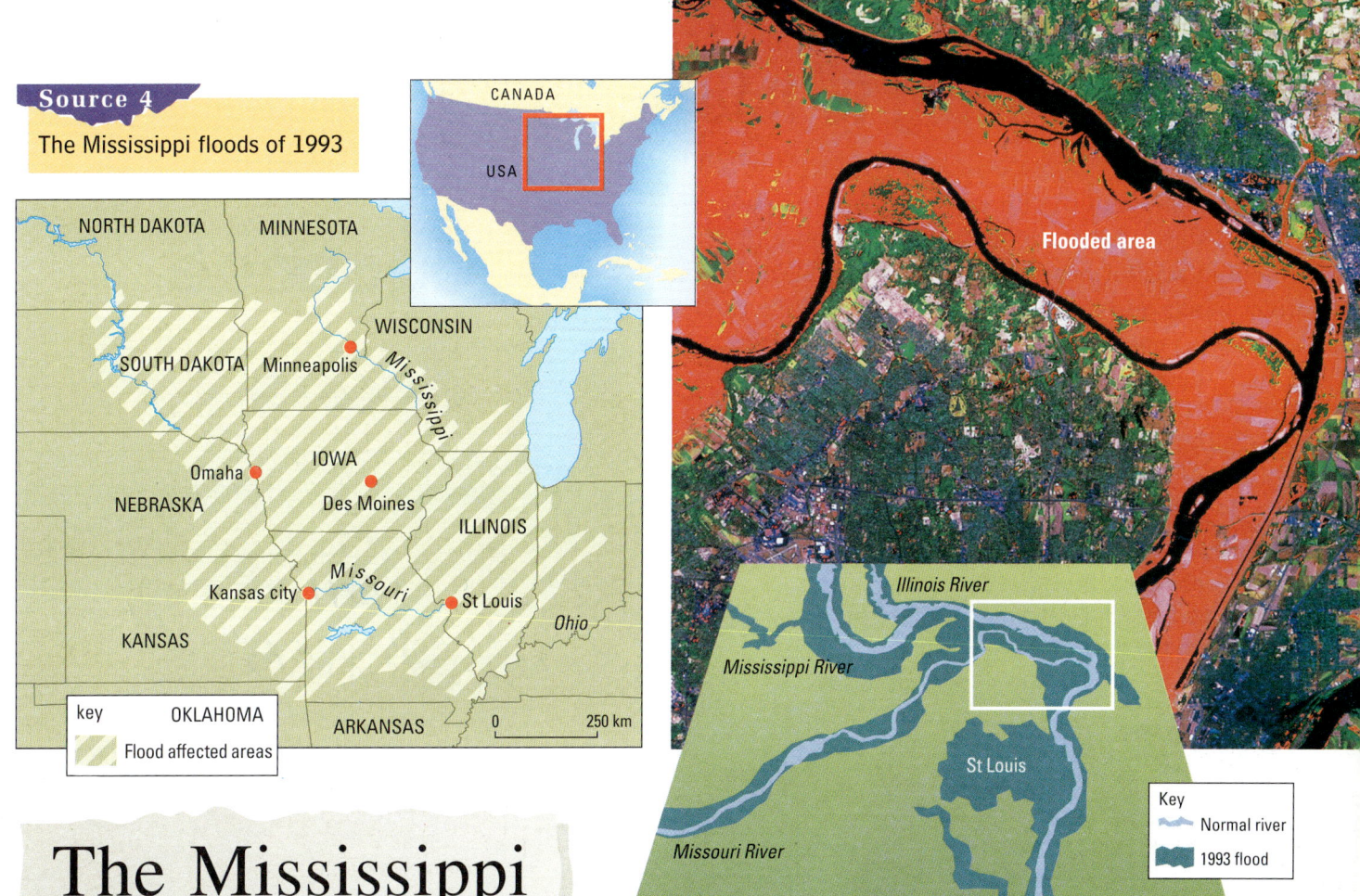

The Mississippi floods of 1993

It rained all spring and summer in the upper Mississippi and Missouri river valleys. 'Boy did it rain.' In some places it rained every day for two months. Most places had two to three times the usual amount of rain. By July an area the size of England was under water. Over 50,000 people were forced out of their homes. Many people were put up in schools and public buildings, which were used as temporary shelters. Fifty people died. Crop losses are estimated over $6 million and damage to property is put at $10 million. What the people in the Mississippi valley are asking is, 'Will they ever stop the Mississippi flooding?'

The flood record of the Mississippi

Date	Flood record	Attempted solutions
1900	Flooding from the meeting with the Ohio to the Gulf of Mexico	Raise the height of the levées
1927	An area up to 150 km wide was flooded and over 200 people died	Increase further the height of the levées. Build dams on tributary rivers such as the Ohio and Tennessee
1937	An area the size of Scotland was flooded and over 250 people died	Make the levées even higher. Line them with concrete. Straighten some of the meanders.

Activity 3

a) Study the flood record of the Mississippi in Source 4. Now write about the different ways in which people have tried to stop the Mississippi from flooding.

b) Why do you think they have not been totally successful?

Group Activity

Make information posters using the heading 'The Big Mississippi Flood of 1993'. Use the information in Source 4 to help you.

Decide first what it is best to include and then share out the work in your group.

Responding to floods

The case-study of the River Mississippi (on pages 14–15) showed that the immediate response to flooding was for people to raise the height of the river banks and to strengthen the sides of the river channel. These actions are taken first in towns where there are more people and property to protect. This helps to justify the high cost of the works (Source 1).

Source 1
The banks of the River Wear in Durham have the types of flood protection you can see along the sides of a river in any town

Source 2
The disadvantages of big dams

Cost of building £ £ £ £ £ £ £
Interest on money borrowed £ £ £ £ £ £ £ £ £
Maintenance work £ £ £ £ £

Before the dam was built — fertile silt — flood

After the dam was built — dam — silt

cost to farmer, damage to the environment — add fertiliser

Before

After — reservoir — dam

In their upper courses many rivers are being dammed at even greater cost. This is called **river basin management**. By building a dam, such as at Cow Green in Upper Teesdale (see page 9), the plan is to hold back the water in times of flood, and to supply water to local houses and industries in times of drought.

There has been a large increase worldwide in the number of big schemes to meet the challenge of flooding. The Thames Barrier is one example (see page 31). What is done more commonly to try to control river behaviour is to build a big dam and large reservoir.

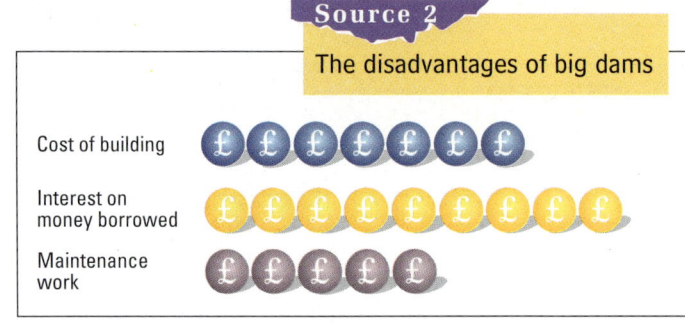

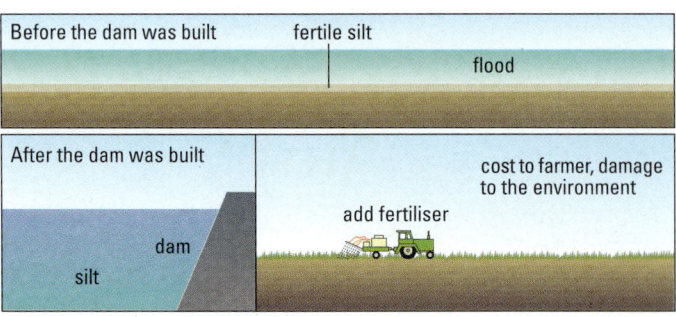

Activity 1

a) Draw a labelled sketch to show the effects that the dam and reservoir would have on the area shown in Source 2.

b) Using Source 2, write about the disadvantages of building big dams.

c) Find out about the methods of flood protection on a river near to you.

Source 3

The Nile Valley in Egypt and the Aswan High Dam

Rivers and floods

Before the Aswan High Dam was built

Amount of cultivated land = 4% of total land area

Nile flood

Farming calendar in Egypt

After the Aswan High Dam was built

Amount of cultivated land = 8% of total land area

crop growing

Farming calendar in Egypt

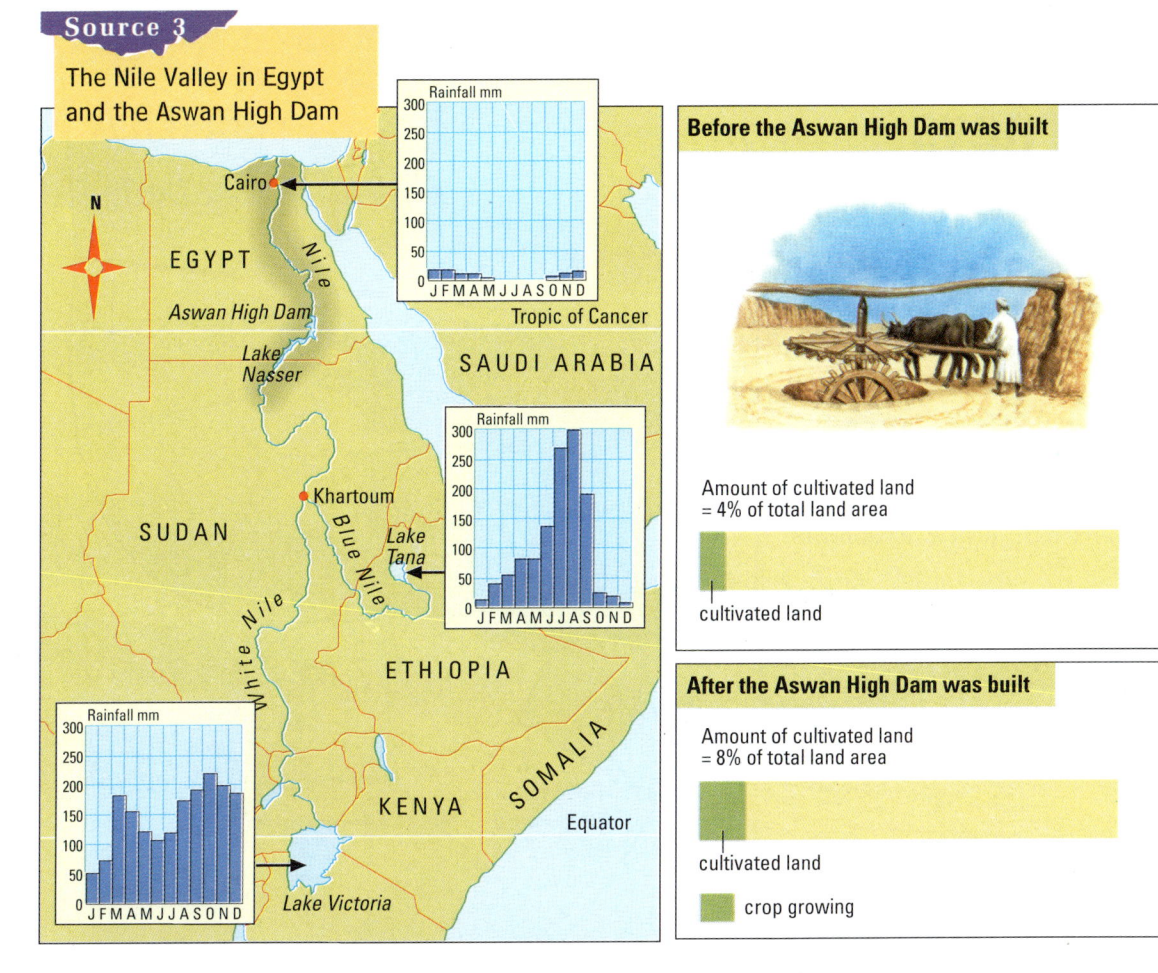

No country knows more about river floods than Egypt. The country has been described as the 'gift of the Nile'. For centuries the River Nile's summer floods watered the land and left behind a layer of fertile silt. The crops grew fast and well in the hot desert sun. Ninety-nine per cent of the people lived on the green strip of land next to the river watered by the Nile flood. Simple methods such as the *shaduf* and *sakeer* (Source 3) were invented centuries ago to raise the water onto the land. Today, however, there is no Nile flood. The Aswan High Dam was built to hold back water in Lake Nasser. This means that the Nile is now a managed river. The water, so essential for life in the desert, now comes from Nile water trapped in a reservoir and not from the Nile's annual flood.

Activity 2

a) Using the map in Source 3, describe the course of the River Nile from its sources to the sea.

b) i) Draw a labelled sketch of the sakeer.

ii) What are the advantages and disadvantages of these compared with large dams for water supplies?

c) Select the information and describe the advantages gained from building the Aswan High Dam.

Activity 3

Use the rainfall graphs on the map in Source 3 to explain why:

a) the Blue Nile supplied more floodwater than the White Nile

b) Egypt's farmers needed the Nile water.

Group Activity

Work in pairs for this activity. Make a list of **either** the advantages **or** disadvantages of dams. Compare your list with a pair taking the opposite view.

River journeys

Group Activity

Work in pairs for this activity. Throw a dice. The lowest score takes river A, the next takes river B. Play the game by continuing to take turns to throw the dice. Go along your river until you reach the finish. The last person to reach the finish must write a report with a title 'Problems along the River'.

Source 2

The two rivers game

RIVER A
START

1
2
3
4 Low water in channel: Miss a turn
5
6
7 Flood water allows rapid progress: Go forward 5
8
9
10 Waterfall delays progress: Go back 4
11
12
13
14 big boulders in river bed: Go back 4
15
16
17
18
19 Fast current: Go forward 3
20
21
22
23 Major waterfall: Miss a turn
24 Land in plunge pool: Go forward 2
25
26 Flood warning: Go back 5
27
28 Dangerous narrow gorge: Miss a turn
29
30

FINISH

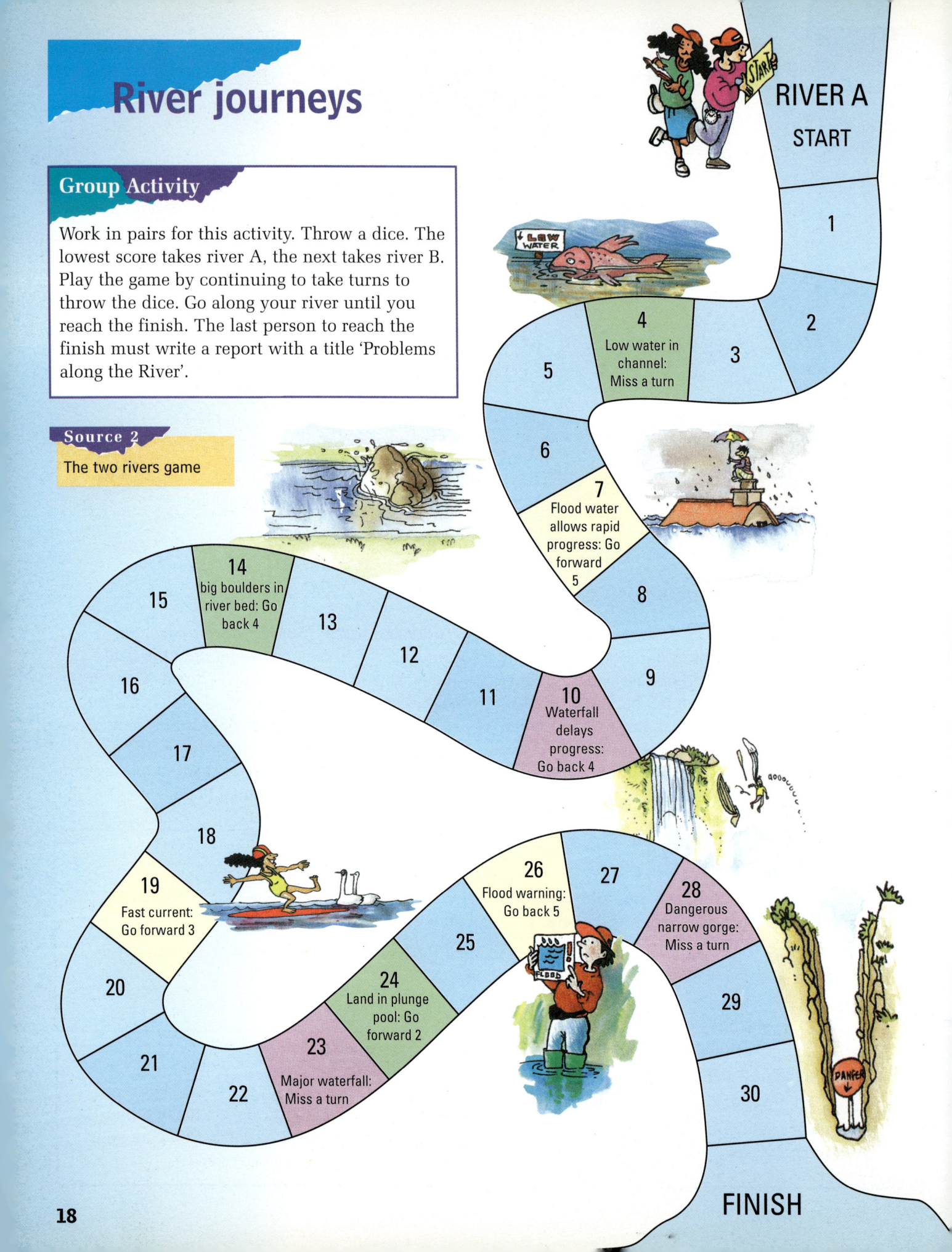

18

2 Rivers Game

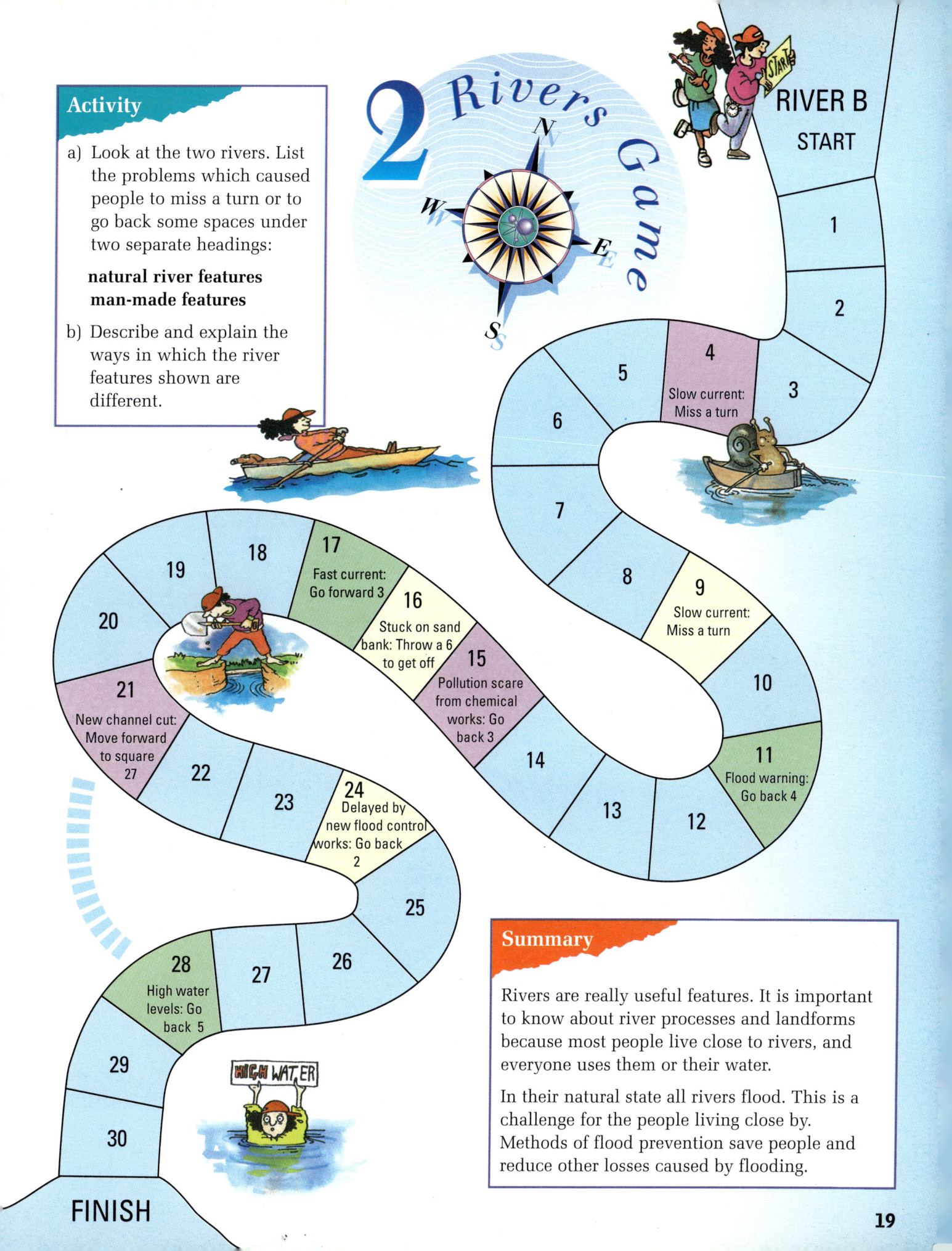

Activity

a) Look at the two rivers. List the problems which caused people to miss a turn or to go back some spaces under two separate headings:

natural river features
man-made features

b) Describe and explain the ways in which the river features shown are different.

RIVER B START

1
2
3
4 Slow current: Miss a turn
5
6
7
8
9 Slow current: Miss a turn
10
11 Flood warning: Go back 4
12
13
14
15 Pollution scare from chemical works: Go back 3
16 Stuck on sand bank: Throw a 6 to get off
17 Fast current: Go forward 3
18
19
20
21 New channel cut: Move forward to square 27
22
23
24 Delayed by new flood control works: Go back 2
25
26
27
28 High water levels: Go back 5
29
30
FINISH

Summary

Rivers are really useful features. It is important to know about river processes and landforms because most people live close to rivers, and everyone uses them or their water.

In their natural state all rivers flood. This is a challenge for the people living close by. Methods of flood prevention save people and reduce other losses caused by flooding.

Coasts

In this unit, you will have a chance to:
- find out about different types of coastline and about coastal landforms
- discover how some coastlines have become a hazard for people
- examine the attempts of people to respond to hazards.

Source 1

Holbeck Hall – a hotel on the north-east coast of England, near Scarborough, in June 1993

- How quickly do you think the coastline in Source 1 changed?
- What part did the sea play in the collapse of the hotel?

Using the coast

The boundary between the land and the sea is called the **coastline**. People use coasts in different ways. Many people visit the coast for holidays. Some industries also prefer coastal locations.

What is the coast?

The sea is constantly moving. At low tide, the edge of the sea may be a long walk from the beach. At high tide, the beach may be crowded because the sea is so close in. The line along the land reached by the highest tides is called the **coastline**. The strip of land between the coastline and low-tide level is called the **shore**. The line reached by the lowest water level is called the **shoreline**. The **beach** is found between the coastline and the shoreline.

Activity 1

Write about a place on the coastline which you have visited, in this country or abroad. Include the following information:

a) where it is – perhaps with a sketch map

b) what the landscape was like – with a sketch, a map or even photos

c) what facilities there were for people.

Activity 2

Source 2 shows three different coastal landscapes. Copy and complete the following sentences to show which coastal landscape would be suitable for each activity mentioned:

a) In coastal landscape _____
   I would sunbathe and go swimming.

b) In coastal landscape _____
   I would go birdwatching on a long walk.

c) In coastal landscape _____
   I would catch a ferry.

Source 2
Different coastal landscapes

Coasts

Activity 3

a) Match the following beginnings to their correct endings:

A cliff is ...	... a sloping area of sand and/or shingle, found on the shore.
The coastline is ...	... the line along the land reached by the highest tides.
The beach is ...	... the strip of land between the coastline and the low-tide level (low-water mark).
The shore is ...	... an area of higher land with a steep slope which is sometimes found behind the beach.

b) What physical features do all coastal landscapes have in common?

c) i) Draw a diagram to show all four parts of the coast

   ii) Describe other types of coastal landscapes you may know about or have seen.

Waves

What makes the waves?

Coastlines are constantly under attack from waves which wear away and remove some of the land. How are waves formed and where do they come from?

Source 1
Two different types of coastline

The wind makes waves and drives them towards the land. A gentle breeze will make a calm sea. Strong winds will cause storm waves. Some of the biggest waves are formed out in the Atlantic Ocean and travel long distances to reach our coast. They grow large because the wind has the time to build the waves up as they travel across the ocean. The distance over which the waves can travel is called the **fetch**.

Activity 1

Look at Source 1.

a) In which photo do you think the sea has more energy?

b) In which photo would it be safe to go swimming?

c) What would the weather feel like in photo B?

Activity 2

a) Using an atlas, measure the fetch across the Atlantic Ocean for waves coming towards England from the south-west.

b) Using Source 2, measure the fetch across the Irish Sea for waves coming towards England from the south-west.

c) Which part of England would be under greater wave attack – the Lancashire coast bordering the Irish Sea or the Cornish coast bordering the Atlantic Ocean? Explain your answer.

Source 2
Wind direction map

Coasts

What are the parts of a wave?

When a wave enters shallow water it changes. Friction with the sea bed makes it slow down. It becomes taller and breaks on to the shore. The water thrown up the beach is called the **swash** and the water draining back down the beach is called the **backwash** (see Source 3A).

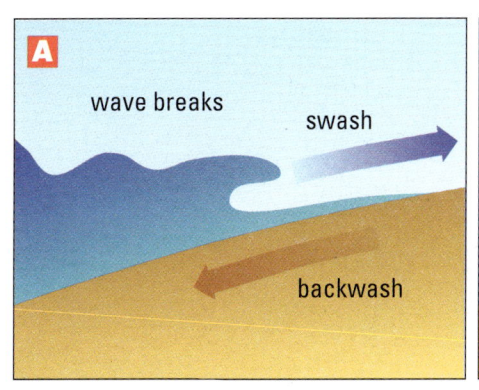

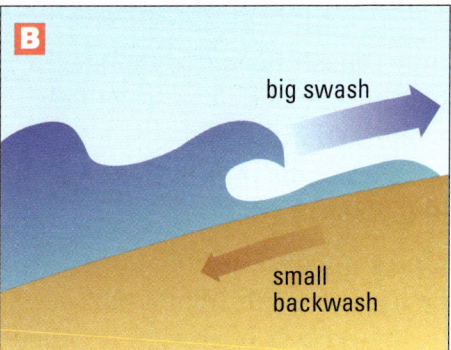

Source 3
Types of waves

A wave breaks — swash — backwash

B big swash — small backwash

C small swash — big backwash

Are there different types of waves?

Waves are formed by the wind. When the wind is gentle, the waves are short and separated out. When these waves break, the swash rushes up the beach as a sheet of water reaching quite high up the beach. Most of the swash soaks into the beach which means that there is very little backwash. These waves are called **constructive waves** (see Source 3B). When the wind is strong, the waves are taller and closer together. When these waves break on to the beach, the water plunges forwards and downwards, so the swash is small. The plunging waves churn up the beach material and the powerful backwash can carry material back down the beach. These are called **destructive waves** (see Source 3C).

Activity 3

a) Copy out the table below. Fill in the boxes to show the differences between constructive and destructive waves. Use a ✓ or an ✗ in columns 1 and 2, and write the answer in column 3.

	1 More powerful swash?	2 More powerful backwash?	3 What these waves do to the beach
Constructive waves			
Destructive waves			

b) Source 4 shows a timescale for the two different types of waves.

i) How many constructive waves will reach the beach per minute?

ii) How many destructive waves will reach the beach per minute?

iii) Which type of waves would you expect to reach the beach in a) stormy weather, b) calm weather?

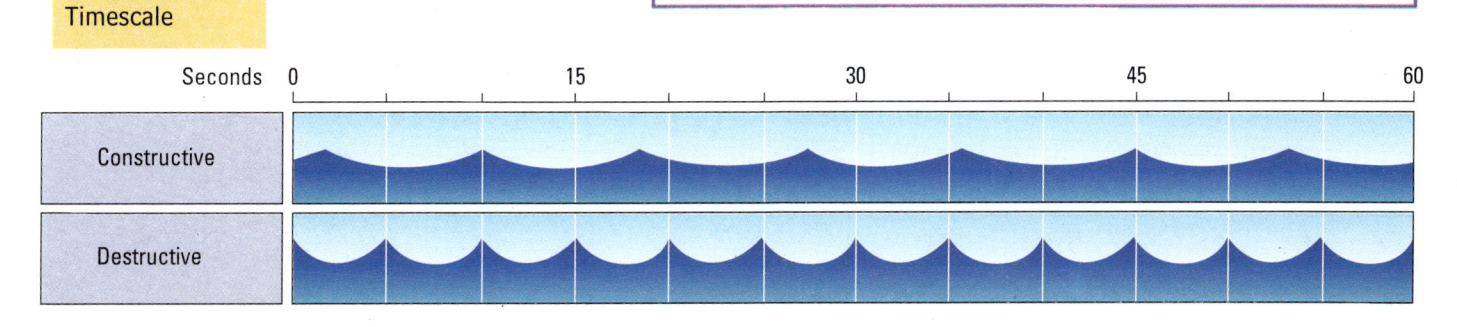

Source 4
Timescale

Seconds 0 — 15 — 30 — 45 — 60

Constructive

Destructive

Eroding the coast

When a wave reaches the shore, friction with the sea bed makes it slow down. It becomes taller and breaks on to the shore. This means that the coast is constantly under attack, being **eroded** away by the sea (See Source 1). The sea can erode the land in three different ways:

1. When waves crash against a cliff, they squash the air in the cracks and holes, hammering it even deeper into the cliff. The wave falls back very quickly, but when this is repeated again and again, a block of rock from the cliff is loosened and falls into the sea. This force of the waves is called **hydraulic action**.

2. Waves have a lot of energy and can pick up sand, pebbles and boulders and crash them against the base of a cliff. When the sea uses these tools along with its force, the process of erosion is called **abrasion**.

3. When blocks of rocks fall off cliffs, they are crashed against other boulders and pebbles as well as against the shore. In this way they are broken into smaller pieces and eventually become sand. This process is called **attrition**.

Source 1
Waves are powerful agents of erosion

Coastal landforms of erosion

Landforms made by the sea eroding the coast fall into three groups:
1. Cliffs and wave-cut platforms (Source 2).
2. Headlands and bays (Source 2).
3. Caves, arches and stacks (Source 3).

Source 2
Cliffs and wave-cut platforms; headlands and bays

Cliffs and wave-cut platforms:
Waves crashing against the base of a cliff undercut it, to form a notch. As the notch slowly gets larger, the overhanging cliff above collapses. A wave-cut platform is left at the base of the cliff.

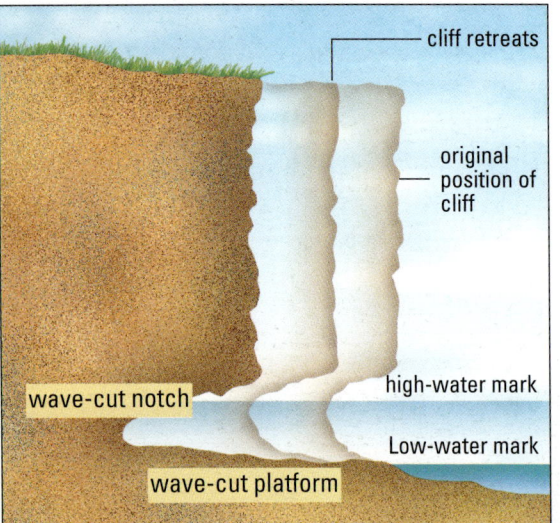

Headlands and bays:
A coastline may have areas of harder and softer rocks. Wave erosion is faster in areas of softer rocks, where a bay will form. Harder rocks are worn away more slowly, so stick out into the sea as headlands.

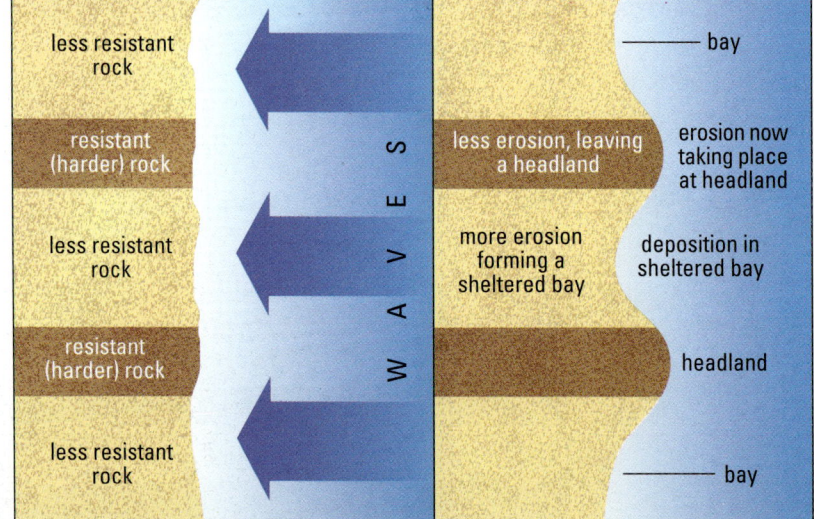

Coasts

Source 3
Caves, arches and stacks

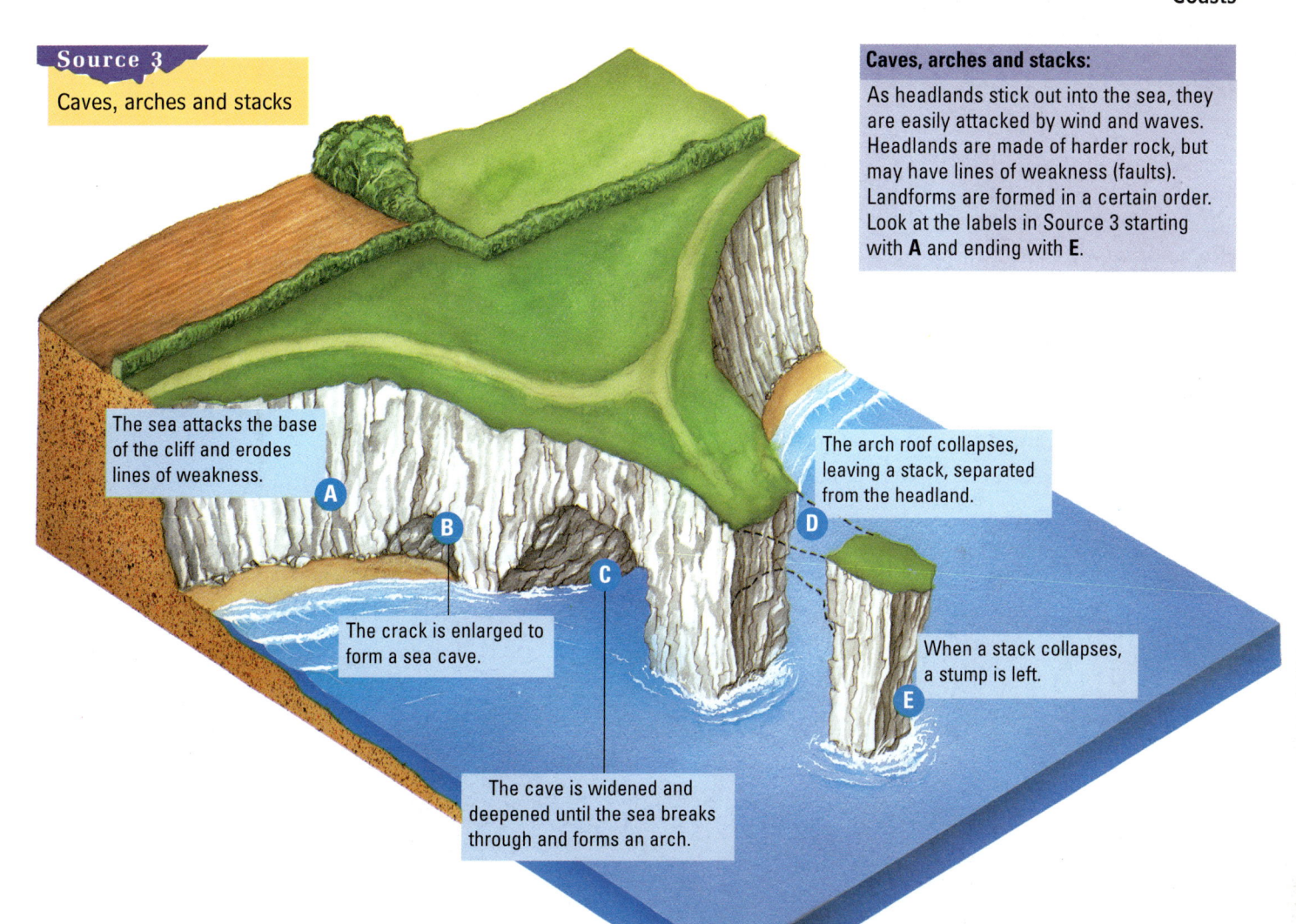

Caves, arches and stacks:
As headlands stick out into the sea, they are easily attacked by wind and waves. Headlands are made of harder rock, but may have lines of weakness (faults). Landforms are formed in a certain order. Look at the labels in Source 3 starting with **A** and ending with **E**.

A — The sea attacks the base of the cliff and erodes lines of weakness.

B — The crack is enlarged to form a sea cave.

C — The cave is widened and deepened until the sea breaks through and forms an arch.

D — The arch roof collapses, leaving a stack, separated from the headland.

E — When a stack collapses, a stump is left.

Activity 1

a) Make a sketch of the photograph in Source 4. Label on to it the following features: cliff, wave-cut platform, arch, stack and stump.

b) Imagine the same coastline in another 5,000 years time. Draw and label what you think the coastline would look like by then.

Source 4
Enys Dodman arch and stack, Land's End, Cornwall

25

Change along the coast

Weathering of rocks takes place in all landscapes, but often takes place under the soil, so that it is difficult for us to see its effects. At the coast, the effects of weathering can be seen at cliff faces.

Weathering is when rocks are broken down by the effects of the weather, plants or animals. The broken-down rocks stay in the same place.

Erosion is when rivers, moving ice, waves or winds pick up the broken rocks made by weathering, move them and use them to wear away the land.

Transport is when the agent of erosion (rivers, ice, waves or wind) moves the broken rocks (or load) from one place to another.

Deposition builds up new landforms from eroded and transported material which is put down somewhere new.

In this way, all these processes which take place at the coast are linked together, as explained in Source 1.

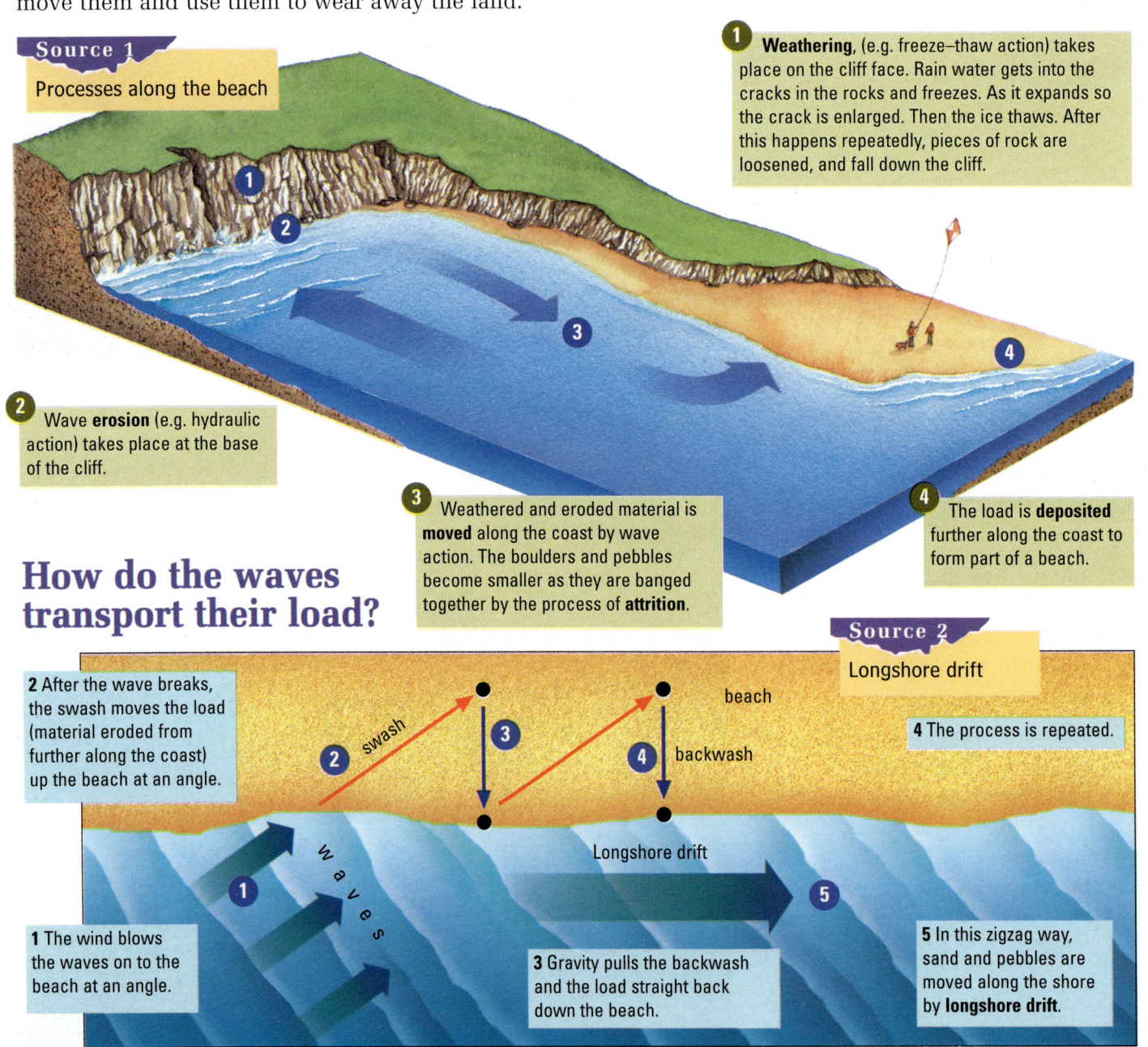

Source 1
Processes along the beach

1 Weathering, (e.g. freeze–thaw action) takes place on the cliff face. Rain water gets into the cracks in the rocks and freezes. As it expands so the crack is enlarged. Then the ice thaws. After this happens repeatedly, pieces of rock are loosened, and fall down the cliff.

2 Wave **erosion** (e.g. hydraulic action) takes place at the base of the cliff.

3 Weathered and eroded material is **moved** along the coast by wave action. The boulders and pebbles become smaller as they are banged together by the process of **attrition**.

4 The load is **deposited** further along the coast to form part of a beach.

How do the waves transport their load?

Source 2
Longshore drift

1 The wind blows the waves on to the beach at an angle.

2 After the wave breaks, the swash moves the load (material eroded from further along the coast) up the beach at an angle.

3 Gravity pulls the backwash and the load straight back down the beach.

4 The process is repeated.

5 In this zigzag way, sand and pebbles are moved along the shore by **longshore drift**.

Coasts

Longshore drift (Source 2) is usually in the direction of the prevailing wind. In Britain this is from the south-west, so material is moved from west to east along the south coast of England. This explains why the pebbles on a Dorset beach are many different colours. Many of the pebbles have been transported long distances from Devon (130 km to the west) and are made of chalk and flint from Devonshire cliffs. Natural processes connect places which are some distance apart. It is impossible for people to change one part of the coastline without affecting other parts of the coastline.

In some holiday resorts, people are worried about longshore drift removing their beach. They build **groynes** (strong wooden fences) stretching into the sea at right angles to the beach. These trap the material moved by longshore drift, so that the beach does not move, but they also give the beach a different shape (Source 3).

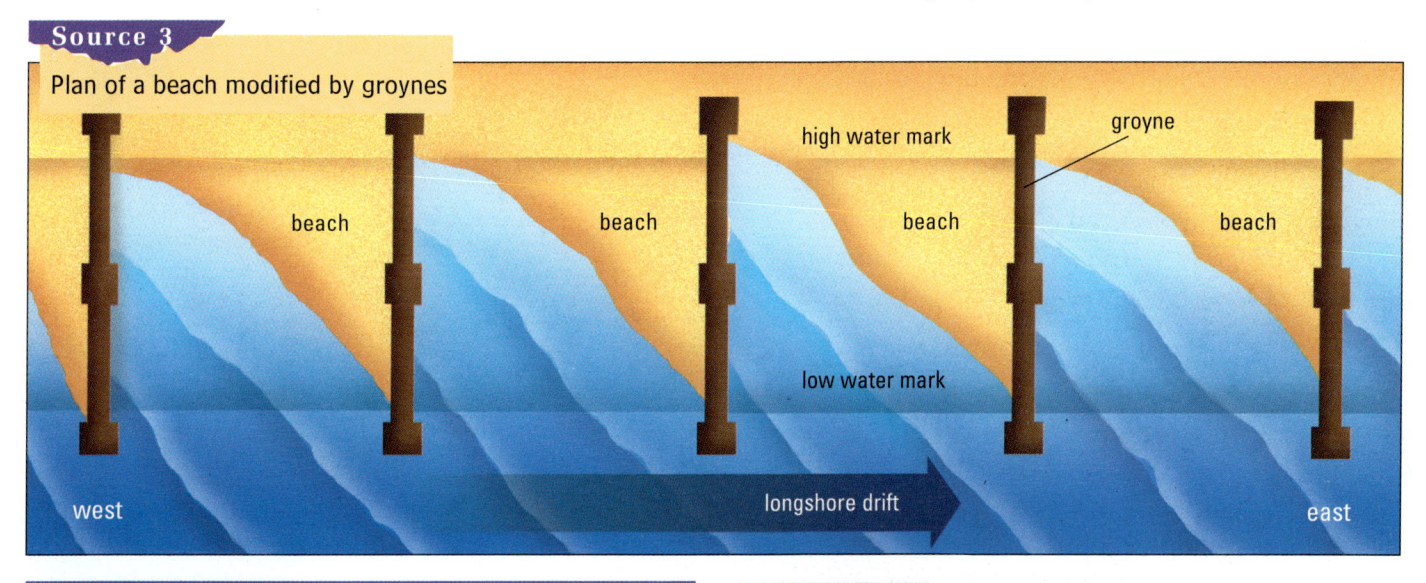

Source 3
Plan of a beach modified by groynes

Source 4
A bay with a wide sandy beach

Activity

a) Make a copy of Source 2 in your book. Complete your diagram by showing how the load will reach the right-hand side of the beach.

   i) Use different colours for swash and backwash.

   ii) Make a key and give your diagram a title.

b) Source 4 shows a bay with a wide sandy beach in the middle. In this case, the waves are blowing on to the centre of the beach X at right angles, but this is not so for the curved parts of the beach (at Y and Z). Make a copy of Source 4 in your book.

   i) Draw on the pattern of swash and backwash in two colours, on both sides of the bay, starting from the points marked 1.

   ii) Explain why the centre of the bay has a wide sandy beach.

Building up the land

Longshore drift moves material along the coast. Constructive waves deposit the pebbles, sand and mud on the coast to form a gently sloping platform called a **beach**. Most beaches rest on wave-cut platforms, between high- and low-water levels. Beaches are continually changed by the waves into different shapes. Shingle beaches usually have steeper slopes than sandy beaches, which are more gently sloping.

Group Activity

In small groups discuss why people on holiday find sandy beaches more attractive than pebble beaches. Make a list of reasons.

The formation of spits

A **spit** is an area of sand or shingle deposited by longshore drift, which can extend at a gentle angle out to sea or grow across a river estuary and make the river change its course.

Source 1 shows how a spit is formed.

The formation of Orford Ness, a spit in East Anglia

The historical maps in Source 2 show how Orford Ness has developed in the last 400 years – relatively quickly for a geographical landform.

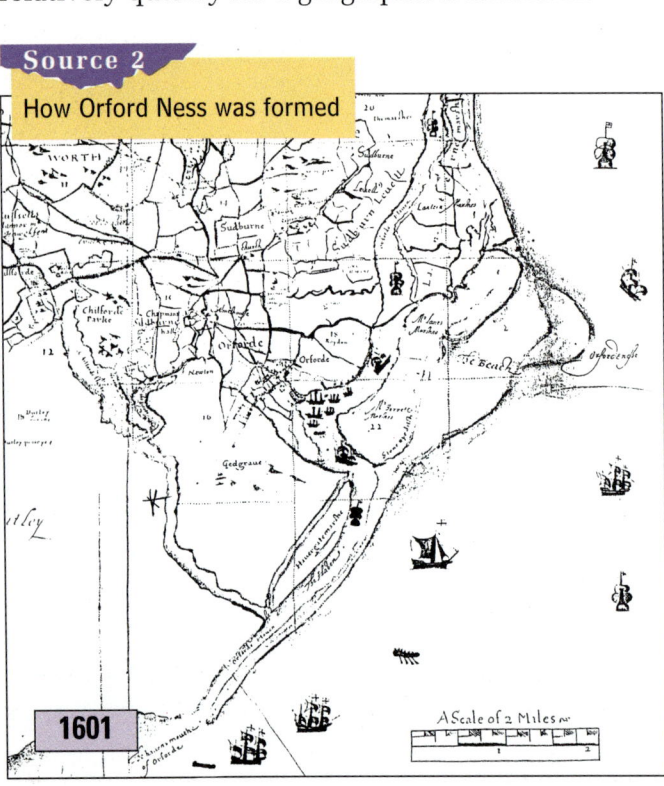

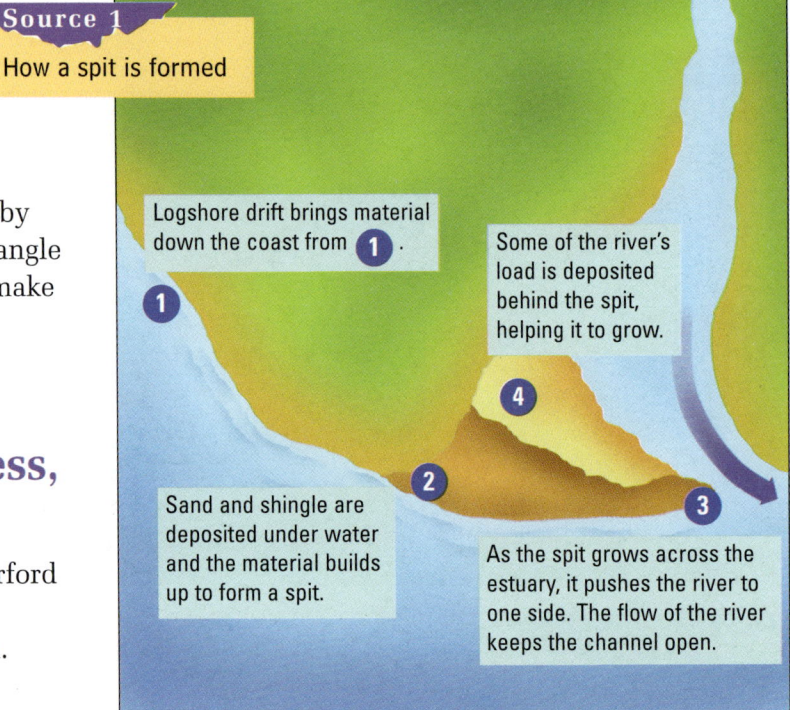

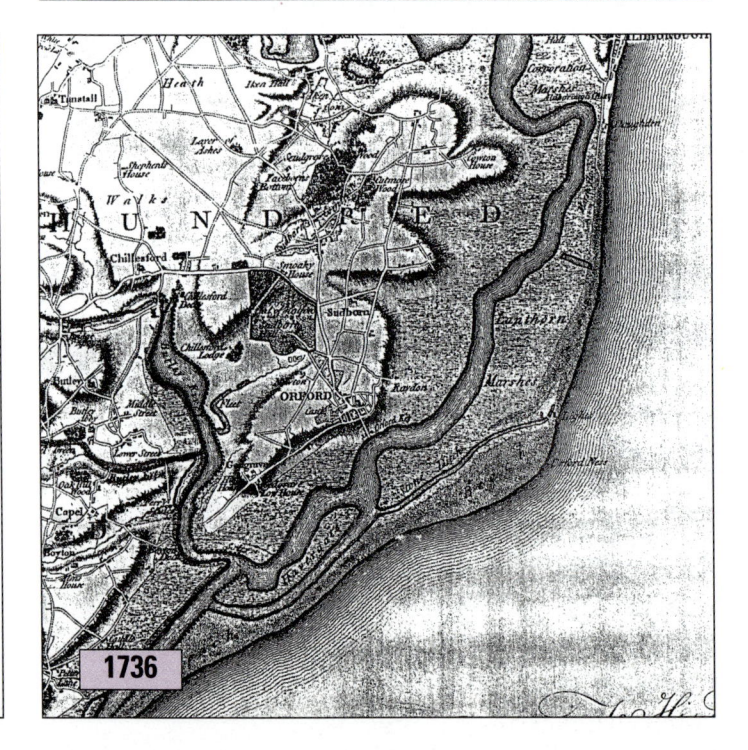

Source 1 How a spit is formed

1. Logshore drift brings material down the coast from **1**.
2. Sand and shingle are deposited under water and the material builds up to form a spit.
3. As the spit grows across the estuary, it pushes the river to one side. The flow of the river keeps the channel open.
4. Some of the river's load is deposited behind the spit, helping it to grow.

Source 2 How Orford Ness was formed

1601

1736

Coasts

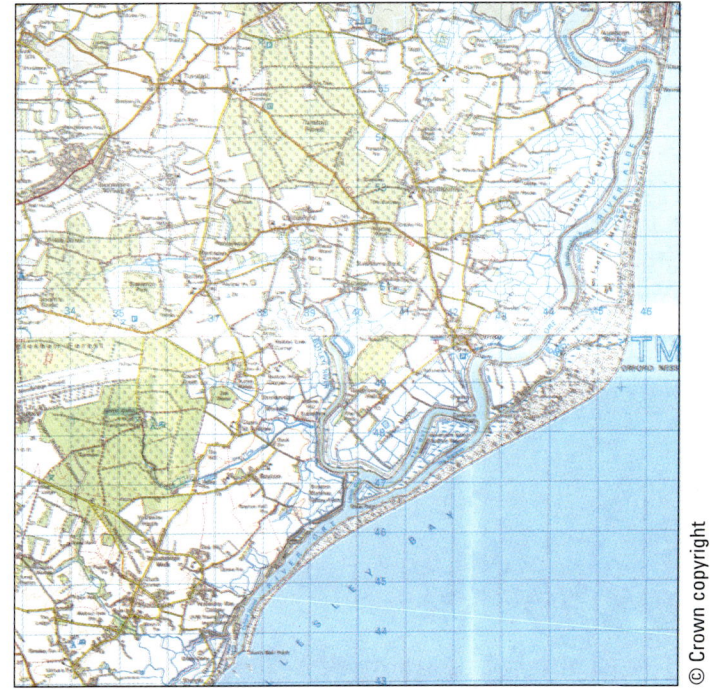

1825

Activity 1

a) Describe how Orford Ness has been formed.

b) Describe and explain what has happened to the River Ore.

Source 3
The coastline of East Anglia

The coastline of East Anglia

The soft, clay cliffs of Norfolk were eroded to provide the material for Orford Ness. Further south, the beaches formed from longshore drift have become places which absorb wave energy and protect the cliffs behind them, as well as providing the east-coast resorts with their famous sandy beaches. However, longshore drift can cause problems for people who want to use the coast for other activities.

At Harwich, dredgers must work hard to keep the port open (Source 3). The sand and gravel they remove from the sea bed is sold to the construction industry. The dredging at Harwich allows so little material to drift southwards along the coast to Clacton that the beaches there are in danger of being stripped away completely.

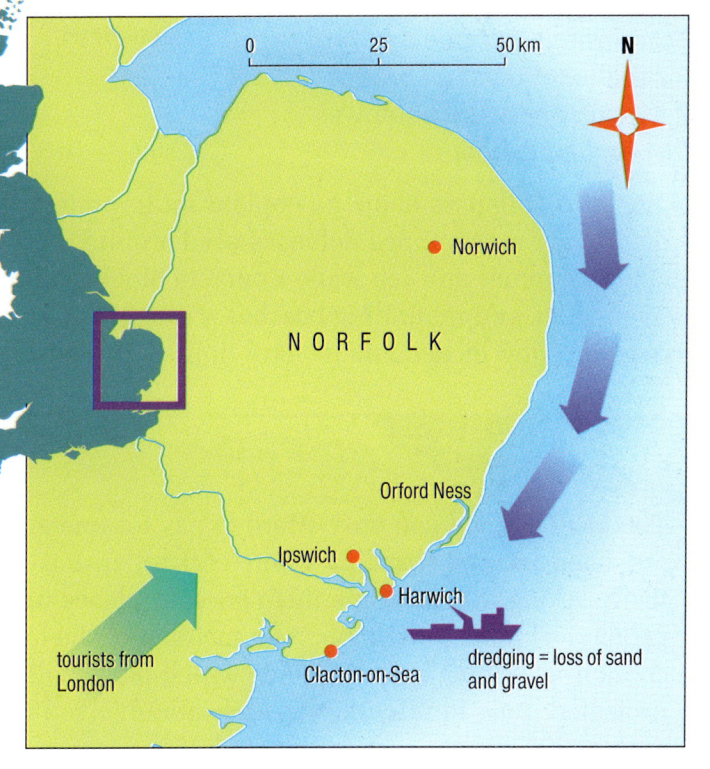

Activity 2

a) How do beaches protect the cliffs behind them from erosion?

b) Clacton already has a sea wall and groynes to try and protect its beach. What else can it do to keep a beach for its tourists?

29

Coastal hazards

Some people retire and move to the coast to enjoy a view of the sea. Many others live and work at the coast – in fishing, factories or tourism. What geographers see as natural processes, can become **hazards** for people in coastal locations (Source 1).

The problem for people who try to manage the coast is how to break out of the vicious circle.

Cliff collapses

The location of the Holbeck Hall Hotel (see page 20) near Scarborough became a hazard for the hotel owners. Source 2 explains how the hotel was lost in a landslide.

When cliff collapses happen people want to protect the coast from further erosion. Sea defences used around our coasts include: groynes and sea walls, concrete blocks, building wave baffles and rebuilding beaches. Protecting the coast is expensive, and local councils have limited budgets.

Source 1 The vicious circle

1. The natural coast free from human use.
2. People start to settle and develop at the coast.
3. People see the coastal processes of erosion and deposition as a threat to existing or future development. People want coastal protection.
4. Coastal defences are built. Dredging of harbours starts. People change the coastal environment.
5. People are protected – but natural processes continue.
6. Heavy storms cause cliff collapse. Storms cause heavy waves which come over the sea wall.

Source 2 The collapse of Holbeck Hall Hotel

Hotel on cliff top. Heavy rain soaked into soft boulder clay making it unstable.

The wet boulder clay slipped down the cliff, taking the hotel with it.

Wave erosion removed the collapsed boulder clay, so the process could start again.

Group Activity

The local council can only afford to pay for one area of sea defences on a coastline where cliff collapse is likely. Along this coastline there are four places which people feel need protection. As a member of the local council, you must help to decide which place will be protected. Bear in mind how people are involved in each place, and the way in which the land is used.

a) Copy the table opposite:

b) Rank the four places in order from 1 to 4, with Rank 1 being the people and place you think should get the sea defences. Discuss your ideas with a partner before making your decision.

c) Give reasons to explain why you made your decision.

People	Land use	Rank	Reason
Local hotel owner	Hotel – popular all year round		
Local dairy farmer	Dairy farm – supplies towns in local area		
Ten house owners – they cannot sell their houses	Ten houses – the opposite side of the road has already slipped into the sea		
Caravan-site owner	Caravan site – next to go is the site shop and land on which ten caravans are parked		

Coastal flooding

In 1953 floods on the east coast of England and in the Thames Estuary caused the deaths of 300 people. Extra high tides and a **storm surge**, caused by low air pressure and a severe northerly gale, pushed sea water southwards and up the Thames Estuary. If the Thames flooded central London, 1.5 million people would be at risk, and homes, shops and offices would be hit. The response was to build the Thames Barrier (Source 3) to protect London from flooding.

Coasts

Places that will flood:
1. Houses of Parliament
2. Westminster Abbey
3. St. Pauls Cathedral
4. National Theatre
5. Royal Festival Hall
6. Buckingham Palace
7. Piccadilly Circus
8. London City Airport
9. Waterloo

Key: Land below 5.4 metres

Places that won't flood:
10. British Museum
11. Hyde Park
12. Albert Hall
13. Harrods
14. Bank of England
15. Stock Exchange

Source 3 The Thames Barrier

Bangladesh is a low-lying country. Source 4 shows the reasons why it is at risk from coastal flooding.

Source 4 Bangladesh

- flat delta lands
- shallow sea due to silt deposited by rivers
- Bay of Bengal (narrow towards the north)
- typhoons from the south-east

Activity

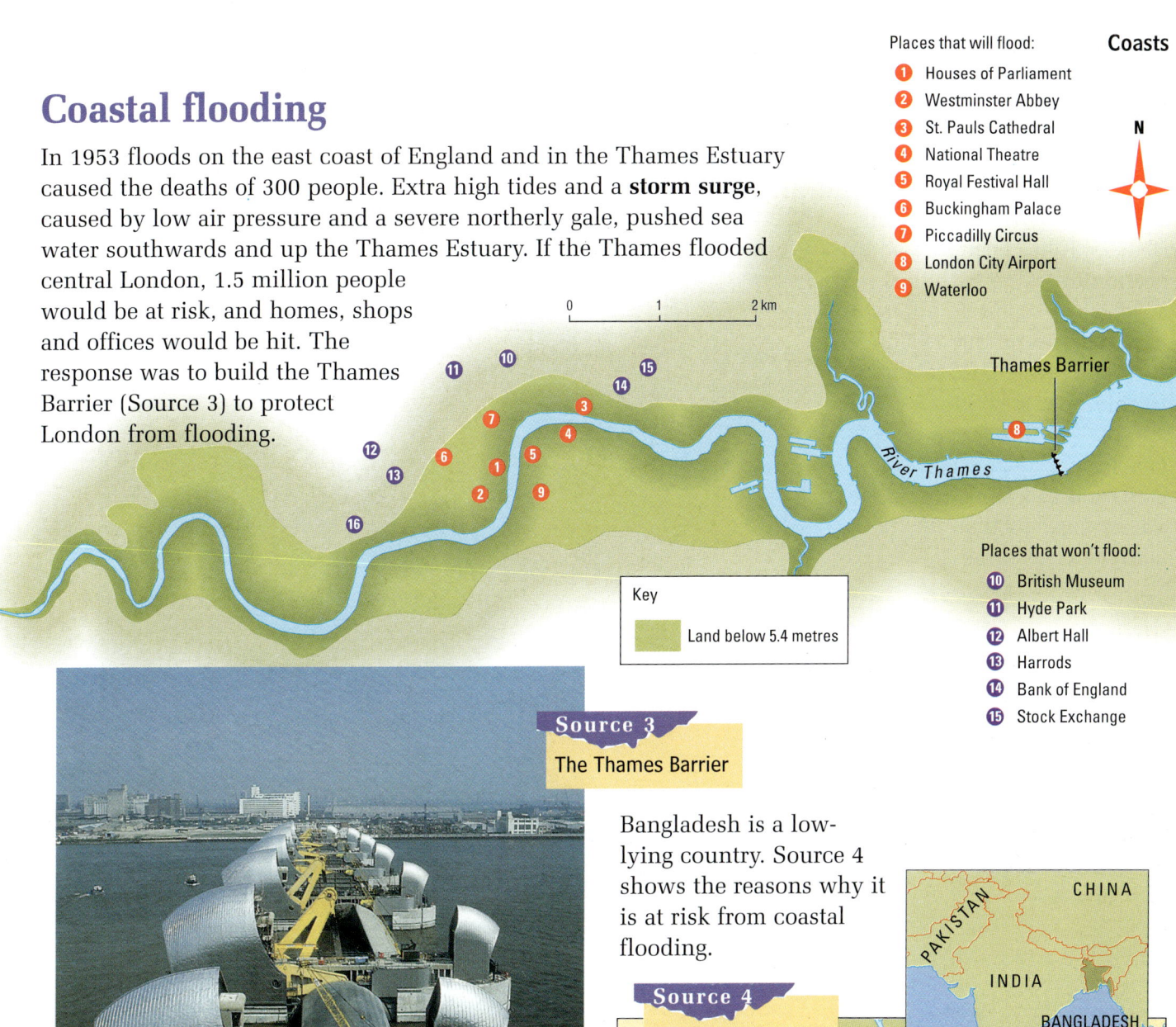

a) Why do so many people live in coastal areas of Bangladesh, knowing that they are at risk from flooding?

b) Why are there no sea defences around the coast of Bangladesh?

31

Focus on the Dorset coast

The Dorset coast has lovely scenery. It has been shaped by erosion, working with the arrangement of three different rock types to produce features such as Lulworth Cove and Durdle Door (see Sources 1 and 2). The three rock types – chalk (hard), sands and clays (soft) and limestone (hard) – are arranged so that they lie along the coastline.

Source 2
Durdle Door, Dorset

Source 1
Lulworth Cove, Dorset

Activity 1

a) In which direction was the camera pointing when the photos of the following places were taken:
- Lulworth Cove
- Durdle Door?

b) Find Durdle Door in square 8080 on the OS map extract opposite.

i) Draw diagrams with labels to explain how this feature was formed.

ii) What landform might develop from Durdle Door in the future?

c) Imagine that you had a caravan to let at the site of Newlands Farm (GR 810807). Using evidence from the map opposite, write a summary of the attractions of the surrounding area which would make a family from a city want to rent your caravan for a holiday.

Coasts

Source 3

Extract from OS map of Purbeck and South Dorset

Activity 2

a) The OS map extract (Source 3) is taken from an Outdoor Leisure Map.

i) Give six figure grid references and names for at least four facilities for tourists.

ii) How is the map helpful for tourists visiting the area? Give map evidence to support your answers.

iii) What problems may result from too many visitors?

b) The map shows Lulworth Camp (square 8381) operated by the Ministry of Defence. There are also Danger Areas (e.g. square 8379) and ranges such as Blindon Range (square 8480).

i) For what purpose do you think the army uses these areas of land?

ii) Do you think it is right to allow military use of this landscape? Explain your view with reference to the map.

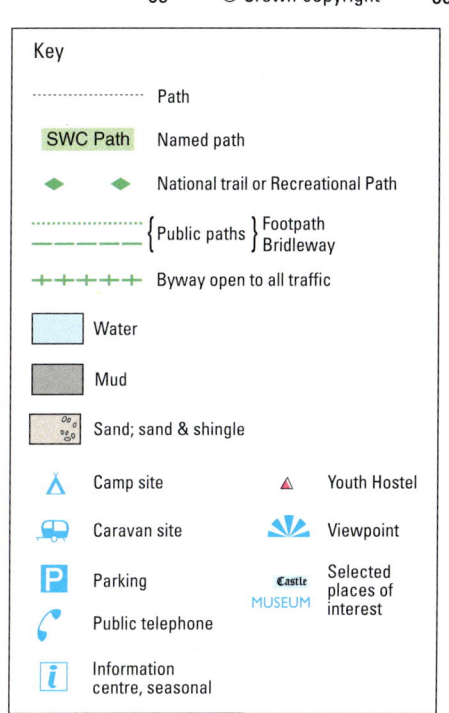

Key

- .... Path
- SWC Path — Named path
- ♦ ♦ National trail or Recreational Path
- .... } Public paths { Footpath
- ------ Bridleway
- +++++ Byway open to all traffic
- Water
- Mud
- Sand; sand & shingle
- ▲ Camp site
- ▲ Youth Hostel
- Caravan site
- Viewpoint
- P Parking
- Castle MUSEUM — Selected places of interest
- ☎ Public telephone
- 𝑖 Information centre, seasonal

33

Coastal development

Settlement and industry like to locate on or near the coast. A large number of different land uses within a small area can cause problems. When there is an opportunity to plan for the development of a coastline, questions need to be asked.

Source 1

Land uses at the coast

Key			
1	Military range	11	Footpaths
2	Coastguard station	12	Pier and entertainments
3	Cliff erosion	13	Seaside resort
4	Power station	14	Beaches
5	Industry using water	15	Caravan and camping site
6	Farming	16	Nature reserve/heritage coast
7	Marina	17	Untreated sewage disposal
8	Fishing		
9	Dredging		
10	Port facilities		

Coasts

Group Activity

Study Source 1 carefully. Work in pairs or small groups.

a) i) Give examples of two manufacturing industries which like coastal locations.

ii) Why does each one like a coastal location?

b) Do all land uses really need to be located at the coast? Some uses need the shoreline, such as a port and leisure use of a beach. Others, like houses and shops, may be attracted to a seafront location, but do they really need to be there?

i) Draw a table like the one below. Divide all the coastal land uses shown in Source 1 into two groups:

- those which **really need** to be at the coast
- those which **do not need** to be at the coast.

Land uses which **really need** to be at the coast	Land uses which **do not need** to be at the coast

ii) Now draw a second table like the one below. Using your list of 'land uses which really need to be at the coast', divide them into two groups:

- those land uses which need to be **on the sea front**
- those land uses which only need to be **near to the sea front**.

Land uses which need to be **on the sea front**	Land uses which only need to be **near the sea front**

iii) Discuss your results in a group of four.

There are no right or wrong answers – but there are different viewpoints. In some cases, local and national interests may be important – in others, conservation arguments may be important.

Activity

Study the imaginary newspaper article in Source 2 and the map on page 33.

a) What is meant by 'an environmentally friendly tourist development'?

b) i) Refer to the map (pages 32–33) to see the types of tourist development which are already found along the Dorset coast. Describe the type of tourist development which you think would be most suitable for the land which is being sold by the MOD (grid squares 8580 and 8581).

ii) Explain how it would have some appeal for all age groups.

Dorset Daily

Development Opportunity - Dorset Coast for Sale

A section of the Dorset coast has unexpectedly become available. The Ministry of Defence has decided that it has no further use for the stretch of coast which includes Mupe Bay, Arish Mell and Worbarrow Bay. The MOD will continue to own and use Lulworth Camp, Blindon Range and Blindon Hill, but will release land for sale in squares 8580 and 8581, so that an access road to the coast can be built. This stretch of previously undeveloped coastline is up for grabs.

A secret would-be purchaser for the access-road land and the area around Arish Mell (GR 854803) is looking for a geographer to come forward with a plan for an environmentally friendly tourist development. The MOD wants to see all development plans before it will sell the land.

Source 2

'Dorset coast for sale'

Ecosystems

Source 1
Life on the African savanna

Plants are important. Animal life on earth, including that of humans, depends upon them. In this unit you will find out about:

- what an ecosystem is
- how climate affects ecosystems
- how ecosystems are being changed by humans.

- What are the different feeding habits of the animals in Source 1?
- Are you aware that all animals, including people, depend directly or indirectly upon plants to feed them?
- Do you realise how important climate is in controlling which plants will grow?

36

Ecosystems

Why are plants important?

An oak tree can live for hundreds of years. The tree is a **habitat** for wildlife. Each year's crop of acorns provides a rich food supply for birds and animals. Dead branches as they drop to the ground can be collected for firewood. When the tree dies its wood can be sawn up. Oak wood is highly prized for making furniture and in the construction industry. For centuries oak beams have supported the roofs of buildings. In other words, the tree is useful to people and to animals while it is still alive, then its wood can be used when it dies (Source 2).

Source 2

The oak tree: a great provider for animals and people

Source 3

World wood usage

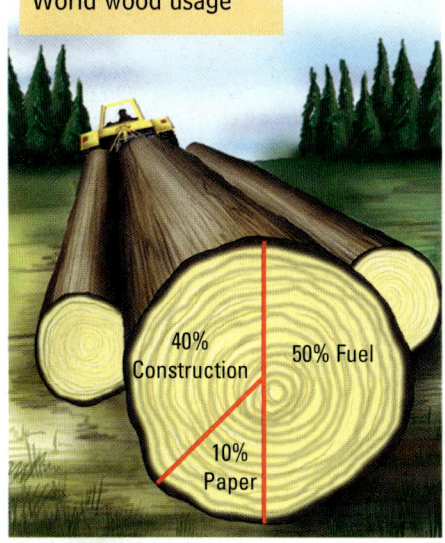

- 40% Construction
- 50% Fuel
- 10% Paper

Group Activity

a) i) In groups of three or four make a list of the different things in the room made of wood.

ii) Make another list of extra things made from wood in and around your home.

b) i) Each person in the group makes a list of their top ten favourite foods.

ii) Put the lists from everybody together under the headings:
- food from plants which grow on the ground
- food picked from trees
- food from animals (although the animals will have fed on plants).

Activity 1

Look at Source 3. Draw bar graphs or a divided bar graph to show world wood usage.

Activity 2

Explain why plants are important to people using the headings: (i) food, (ii) raw materials, (iii) energy supplies.

Natural ecosystems

An **ecosystem** is a living community of plants and animals which are related to the natural (physical) environment (Source 1).

The sun provides the energy which drives the system. Climate is an important feature of the natural environment. This is because plants need warmth and moisture for growth. Soil is also important. The rock below the ground surface weathers to give soil. It is from the soil that the plant roots can find many of the **nutrients** to feed the plants and make them grow.

Source 1

Example of an ecosystem: oak woodland

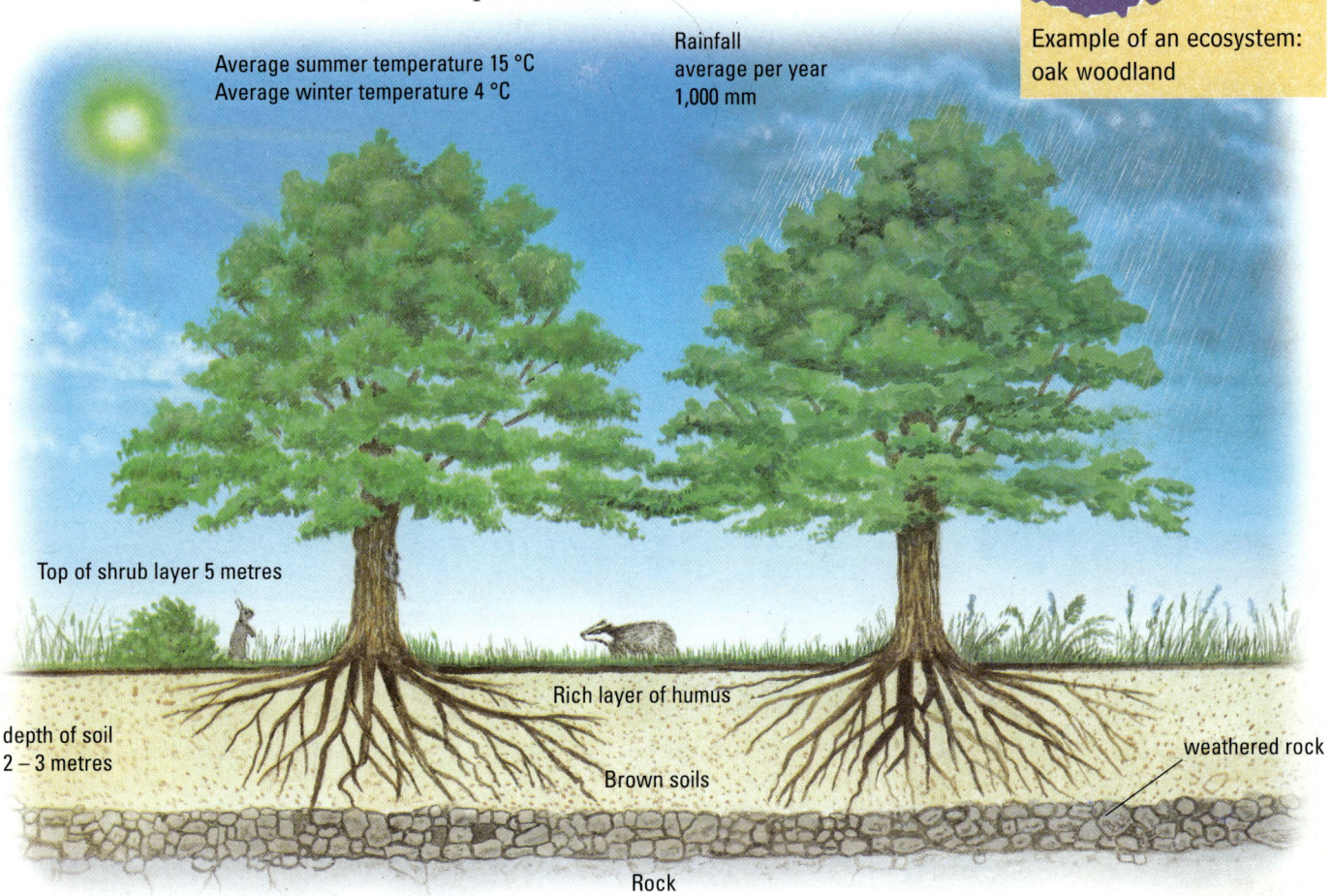

Average summer temperature 15 °C
Average winter temperature 4 °C

Rainfall average per year 1,000 mm

Top of shrub layer 5 metres

depth of soil 2 – 3 metres

Rich layer of humus

Brown soils

weathered rock

Rock

Activity 1

a) Using Source 1, write about the features of the oak woodland ecosystem using the following headings:
  - vegetation cover
  - climate
  - soil.

b) Draw your own labelled sketch to show the main features of the oak woodland ecosystem.

Most plants live in **competitive communities** in which there is fierce competition between plants for light, water and nutrients. There is a simple rule – the taller the plant, the more **dominant** it is. Oak trees were the dominants in many British woodlands. Other plants were shaded out so they had to develop a different life style. If you go into a natural oak woodland in late spring, you can smell the wild garlic and see the carpet of bluebells on the ground. Both flower while there is plenty of light on the floor of the woodland before the oak trees come back into leaf.

Ecosystems

The most competitive communities of plants are found in the tropical rainforests (Sources 2 and 3). There is as much competition at the top of the forest as there is at the bottom. The photograph for Source 2 was taken 50 metres above the ground at the top of a tall tree in the rainforest in Ecuador. If you think about it, it is an ideal place for a 'garden', with the plants having first call on the sunlight and rain water.

Part of the ecosystem idea is that one element within it depends upon another. When plants die, they **decay** and **decompose**. The nutrients that were used to make them grow are returned to the soil to be **recycled** and used again by the new plants which have taken their place. Only recently have humans shown much interest in recycling to conserve the earth's resources, but ever since plants existed, nature has recycled.

Source 2
Top of the forest in Ecuador

Source 3
Forest floor in Brazil. Brazil nut shells are on the forest floor

Source 4
Nutrient recycling

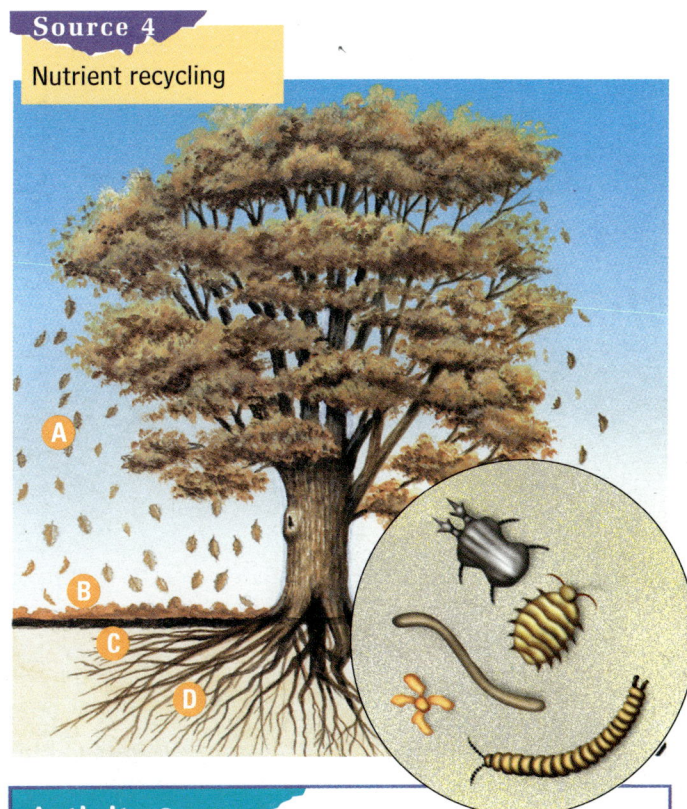

Activity 3

a) Using Source 4 to help you, draw a large labelled diagram to show how nutrients are recycled by nature.

b) i) Name two types of recycling organised by people.

ii) Explain why people are at last showing more interest in recycling things.

Activity 2

a) Describe what plants need for growth.

b) Explain how and why plants compete with one another.

Decay: leaves rot on the forest floor.
Decomposition: material is broken down to release the nutrients.
Nutrients: food sources for plants.
Recycling: use more than once.

How does climate affect vegetation?

Within an ecosystem, the vegetation is often considered to be the most important element. This is because plants are the great **producers** of food. All animals are **consumers** because they need plants for their food. The element in the ecosystem which has the most influence on what type of vegetation is found in an area is climate. Plants have different needs for water and warmth.

Activity 1

Choose two different types of vegetation one from Source 1 and the other from Source 2:

a) draw neat sketches and add labels using the information given about the vegetation

b) describe the features of the temperature and rainfall.

c) explain how the climate affects the vegetation.

Source 1
Vegetation and climate in temperate latitudes

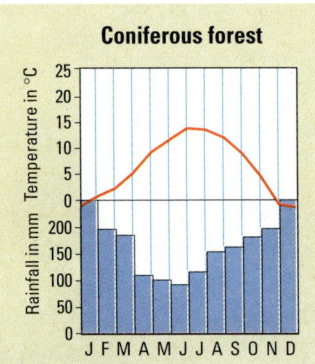

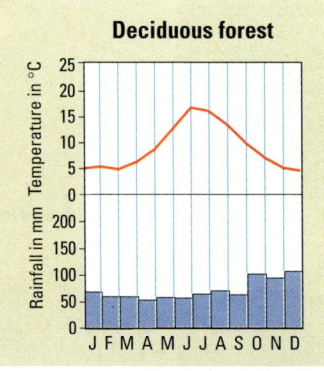

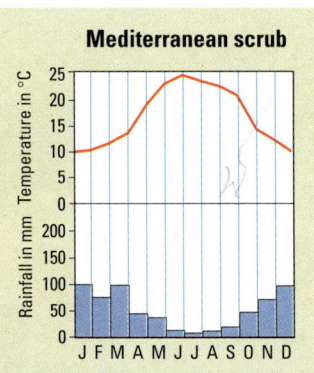

	Coniferous forest	Deciduous forest	Mediterranean scrub
Features of the vegetation	Evergreen trees; cone shaped; up to 20 metres high; needle leaves; only a few types of trees, e.g. fir, pine and spruce.	Trees lose leaves in winter; up to 25 metres high; broad leaves; layer of plants on forest floor; trees such as oak, beech and horse chestnut.	Evergreen trees; up to 15 metres high; small hard leaves; sweet-smelling plants such as lavender; trees such as cork oak and olive.
Adaptations to climate	Shape of trees allows them to withstand snow and cold winds	Winters too cold for growth so they lose their leaves in autumn	Small hard leaves and thick barks to reduce water loss in summer.

Ecosystems

> ### Activity 2
>
> Assuming that the growing season for plants is:
> - a monthly temperature above 6° C, and
> - a monthly rainfall above 50 mm in temperate latitudes and above 100 mm in the tropics
>
> a) from each of the climate graphs work out when the growing season is and how long it lasts
>
> b) show how the length of the growing season affects the vegetation.

> ### Group Activity
>
> Form groups of four for this activity. Imagine the group is going to make an overland trek from Braemar in northern Scotland to Kisangani in Zaire (almost on the Equator).
>
> a) Use an atlas and plot the route on an outline map between the two places named. Name the countries you would pass through.
>
> b) Each person in the group chooses a month at different times of the year. For your month, give the temperature and rainfall conditions for the places along the route.
>
> c) Put all the climatic information together from the group members. Decide upon one month for making the trek. Give reasons for your decision. What different kinds of clothes would you need to take with you?
>
> d) Give details about the changes in vegetation you would expect to find along the route.

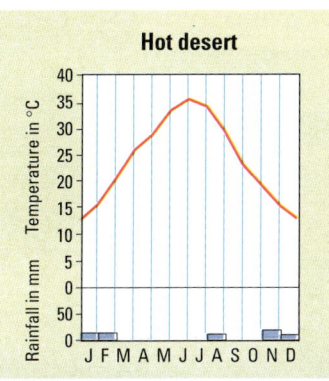

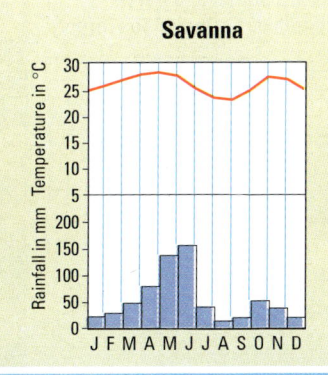

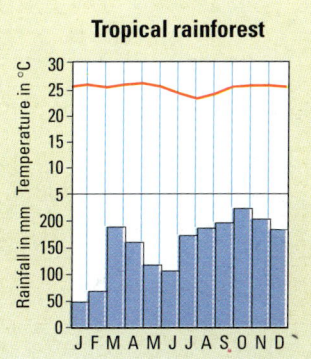

Source 2
Vegetation and climate in tropical latitudes

	Hot desert	Savanna	Tropical rainforest
Features of the vegetation	Small plants with thorns; plants with very deep roots; large areas of bare ground with no vegetation cover.	Tall grasses up to 3–4 metres high; trees dotted around; trees up to 15 metres high; trees are deciduous; trees such as the baobab and the acacia.	Dense evergreen jungle; 4 or 5 different forest layers; tall trees up to 60 metres high such as teak and mahogany; many different types of tree; vines and creepers everywhere.
Adaptations to climate	Deep roots to seek out underground supplies of water; thorns to reduce water loss.	Trees lose leaves in dry season; thick trunks and thorns reduce water loss.	Continuous growth with constant high temperatures and rainfall.

Using ecosystems

At one time humans were no different from other animals; they collected wild plants or hunted wild animals for food. With time, however, people developed the knowledge and the tools to produce their own food. What were once wild plants, such as barley and rice, are now grown as crops. What used to be wild animals, such as cattle and sheep, are now farm animals.

Farmers are now the producers of the food we eat, but the crops and animals they farm originally came from the plants and animals of the world's natural ecosystems. Climate still affects what farmers in different parts of the world can grow. Source 1 gives some information about farming and food in Brazil – a country with a hot and wet tropical climate.

In Cyprus, which is much drier, irrigation water is needed to grow many crops. Much of the drier land is used to graze sheep and goats (Source 2).

Source 1
Farming and food in Brazil

Bananas are made into flour and chips. They replace wheat and potatoes which don't grow well in the tropics. Green bananas are boiled and eaten as a vegetable.

Source 2
Grazing sheep near Lara in North West Cyprus

Activity 1

a) With the help of sketches, describe some of the features of farming in Brazil.

b) Why are bananas such a useful crop in Brazil?

Ecosystems

Source 3

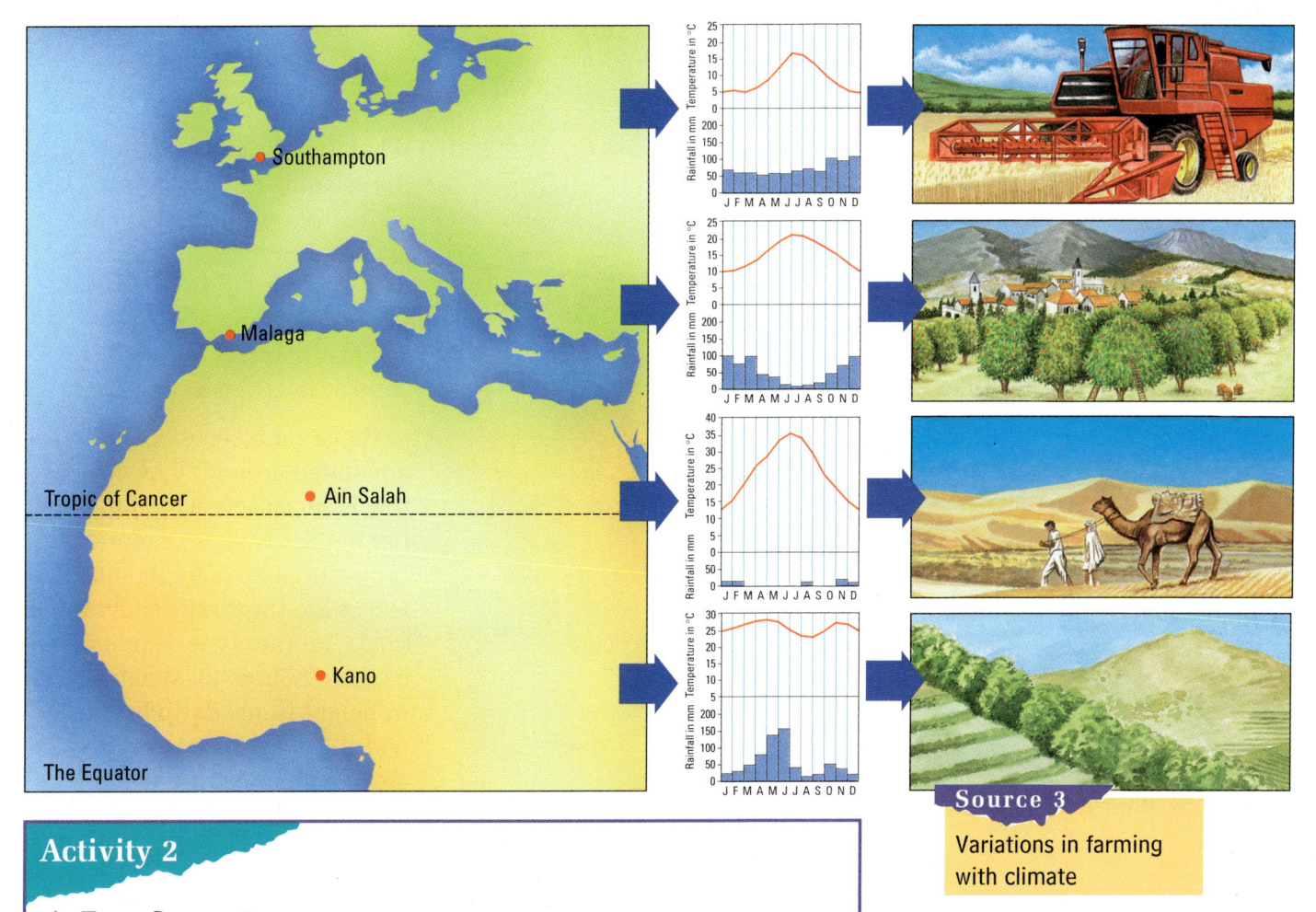

Variations in farming with climate

Activity 2

a) From Source 3

   i) describe what it shows about farming in the United Kingdom

   ii) write about the way farming changes as you move south from the UK towards the Equator

b) Draw a labelled sketch of farming in Egypt using the photograph in Source 4.

Group Activity

a) Work in groups of three or four. Using atlases, try to answer the following questions.

   i) Why is the climate in the UK good for making the grass grow?

   ii) Why is the climate in the Mediterranean better for fruit growing than that in the UK?

b) Use other sources of information to try to answer these questions:

   i) How is the camel adapted to living in the desert?

   ii) What different food and drinks can be made from the vines, olives and oranges grown in Mediterranean regions?

Source 4

Farming in the desert in Egypt

The savanna ecosystem

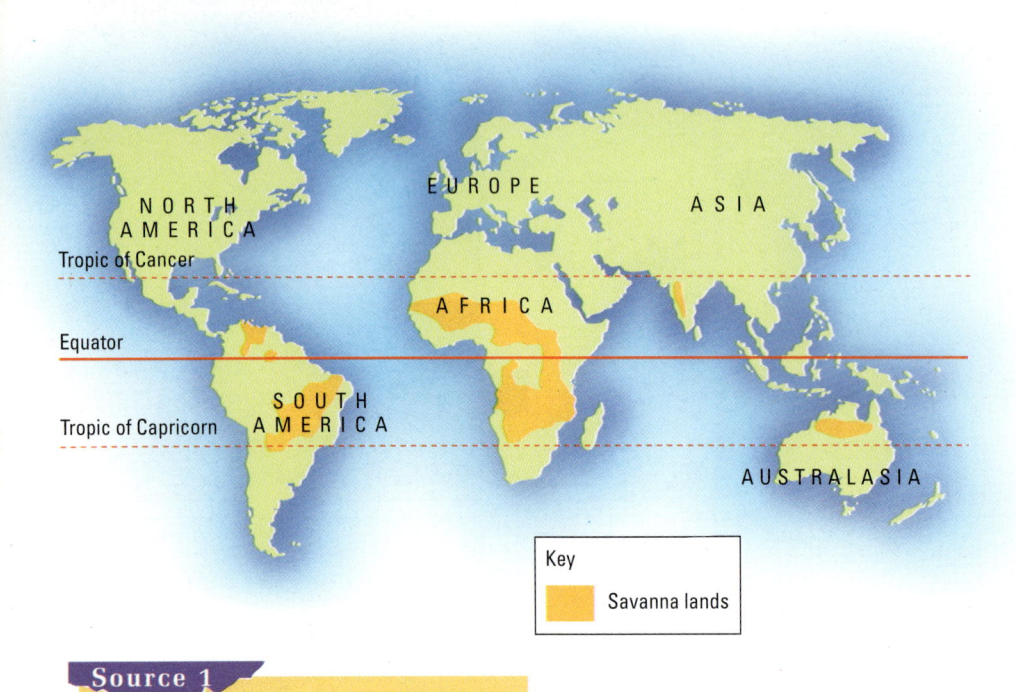

What makes the vegetation in the savanna ecosystem so distinctive is the mixture of grasses and trees. The grasses may grow so tall in the wet season that they are called 'elephant grasses' – almost high enough to cover an elephant!

In the savanna ecosystem, trees are dotted around. One type of tree is the acacia which has a flat top to give it an umbrella shape; unbelievably its thorny leaves are the giraffe's favourite food. Another type of tree is the baobab (Source 2). What it lacks in height it makes up for in width! It may be 9 metres around its huge trunk – quite a waistline.

Source 1
The world distribution of savanna lands

Source 2
The baobab tree

Activity 1

Look at Source 1. Write out the passage below and fill in the gaps using each of these words once in the correct place:

Cancer	largest
Europe	North
horse-shoe	south

The world distribution of savanna lands

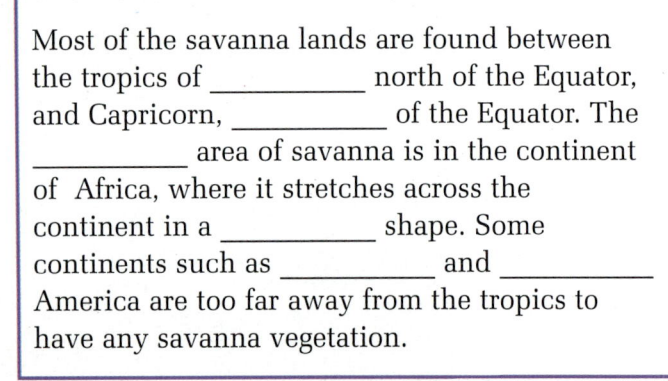

Most of the savanna lands are found between the tropics of _____ north of the Equator, and Capricorn, _____ of the Equator. The _____ area of savanna is in the continent of Africa, where it stretches across the continent in a _____ shape. Some continents such as _____ and _____ America are too far away from the tropics to have any savanna vegetation.

Activity 2

From the photograph on page 36 and Sources 2-4 on pages 44-45 draw a labelled field sketch to show the features of savanna vegetation.

Ecosystems

Source 3

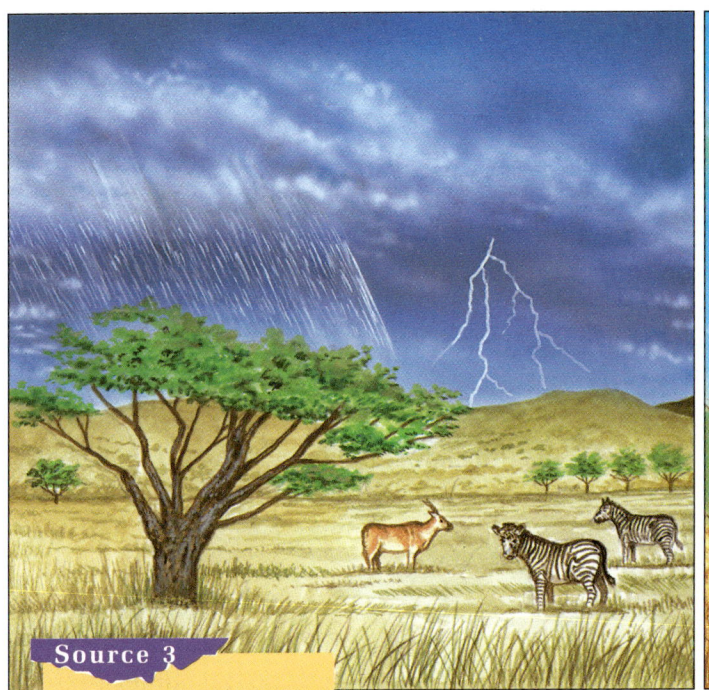

Wet and dry seasons in the savanna

Source 4

How plants adapt to drought in the savanna

Loses leaves in the dry season to reduce water loss

A lot of wood and little leaf

Thorns to reduce water loss

Leaves lost in dry season

Thick spongy bark to hold water and stop water loss

Deep roots

Acacia tree

Baobab tree

The savanna climate is hot. The average monthly temperatures are between 20°C and 35°C. Its coldest month is warmer than the warmest month in Britain. The annual total of rainfall is between 500 and 1500 mm, similar to that in Britain. The big difference is that all the rain falls in only a few months of the year (Source 3). When it is wet the plants love it. Grasses shoot up. Leaves return to the trees. In the dry season, however, the landscape changes from green to brown as everything is baked by the scorching tropical sun. The trees only survive because of their adaptations to drought (Source 4). In the hot dry season the big waistline of the baobab tree is a life saver.

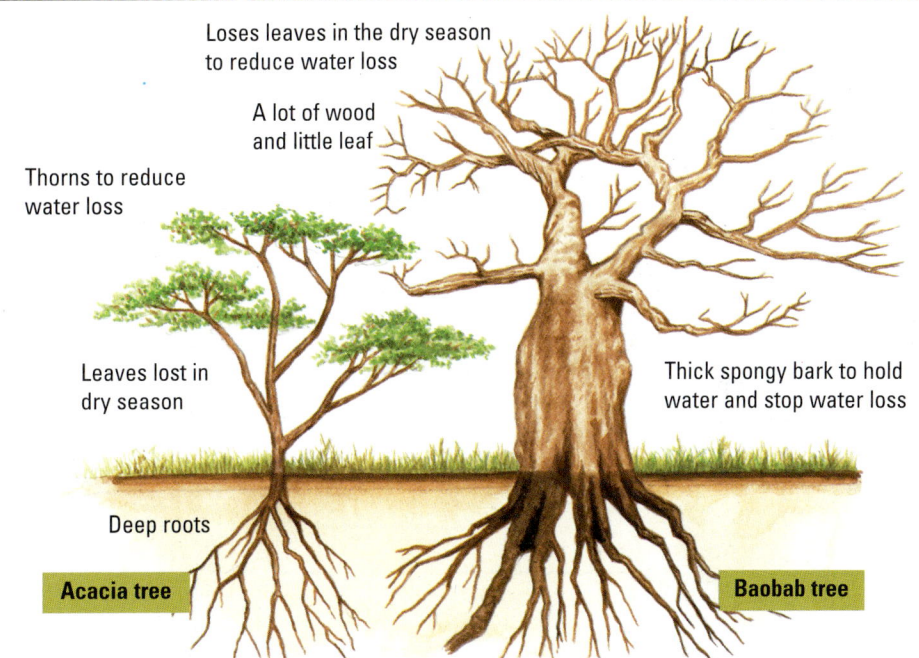

Activity 3

a) With the help of labelled sketches describe how the weather, vegetation and landscape in savanna lands changes from the wet season to the dry season.

b) Using information from earlier in the unit as well

i) describe the differences between the vegetation of the deciduous forest ecosystem in Britain and the savanna ecosystem in Africa

ii) suggest reasons why they are different.

45

The changing savanna

So far we have just looked at two elements in the savanna ecosystem – vegetation and climate. However, the savannas in East Africa are also home to many animals. There are great herds of grass-feeding animals – called **herbivores**. You may have seen wildlife programmes showing the great herds of antelope, zebra and wildebeest. These grass-feeding animals are a vital part of the **food chain** which the savanna vegetation supports (Source 1). They are the food supply for the hunting animals – the meat eaters, or **carnivores**.

The energy stored in plants is passed on to the animals that eat them. The animals use energy for body heat, to move around for new grass and to try to escape from other animals which could kill them. Only a small amount of energy is stored as flesh and bone, so only a small amount is passed on when the animal is eaten. Some carnivores, such as lions and hyenas, hunt in packs, but you may have noticed that the numbers of those doing the hunting are much smaller than those being hunted. A lot of grass-eating animals are needed to support a few meat-eating animals (Source 2).

Source 1
Food chain in the savanna ecosystem in East Africa

CARNIVORES e.g. wild dog, hyena, chetah, lion

HERBIVORES e.g. giraffe

HERBIVORES e.g. antelope, gazelle, zebra, wilderbeast

TREES and GRASSES

- Consumers
- Consumers
- Food producers

Source 2
Trophic levels in the savanna ecosystem

- Humans
- Carnivores
- Herbivores
- Vegetation

Activity 1

a) Explain the differences between a herbivore and a carnivore.

b) Using Source 1, give two examples of a food chain in the savanna ecosystem.

c) Explain why people going on safari to East Africa see more zebra than lions.

Food chain: the energy from plants is passed along a chain of living things.

Trophic level: food level.

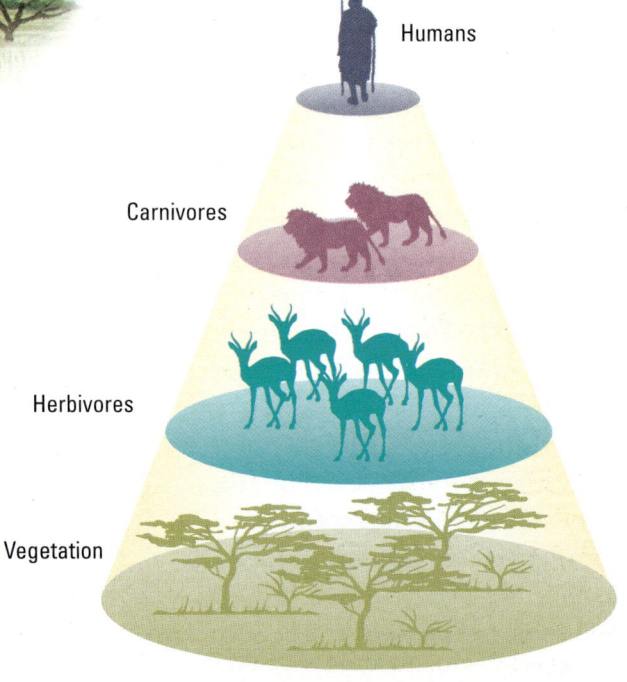

Ecosystems

Source 3

Land uses in the savanna lands of East Africa

Labels on illustration: rock outcrops, dry river bed, cattle and goats, shifting cultivation, pool in river bed, maize, water-carrying, millet, village, soil erosion, bush fallow

Source 4

Elephants on the move. Notice the umbrella shape of the acacia tree.

You may have noticed that humans have been placed on the top food level in Source 2. Humans are **omnivores**. This means that they eat both plants and meat. People have the power and the knowledge to change ecosystems. The native peoples burn off the dry vegetation each year. This encourages new grass growth once the rains arrive, but fire destroys tree saplings. The result is fewer trees. Growing crops and wild animals do not mix. A herd of elephants crashing through the savanna vegetation isn't going to do much good to a corn field along its path! Birth rates are high so people need more land for farming. The local people trap and shoot wild animals. The result is more people and fewer wild animals.

Group Activity

Work together in groups of three or four.

a) List the different land uses shown in Source 3.

b) Now find the evidence that the growth in population has had a bad effect in the area.

c) What might the area have looked like about 100 years ago when there were many fewer people? Write down your ideas.

d) Using these ideas, draw your own version of Source 3 showing what the area might have looked like 100 years ago.

47

The challenge of preservation and conservation

Source 1 shows what has happened to the savanna ecosystem in some parts of Africa. Pressure from greater numbers of people is changing and damaging the natural savanna ecosystem. People are also trying to achieve a better quality of life.

Activity

With the help of labelled sketches, explain how one change can lead to another until the ecosystem is destroyed.

Source 1
Change and damage to the savanna ecosystem

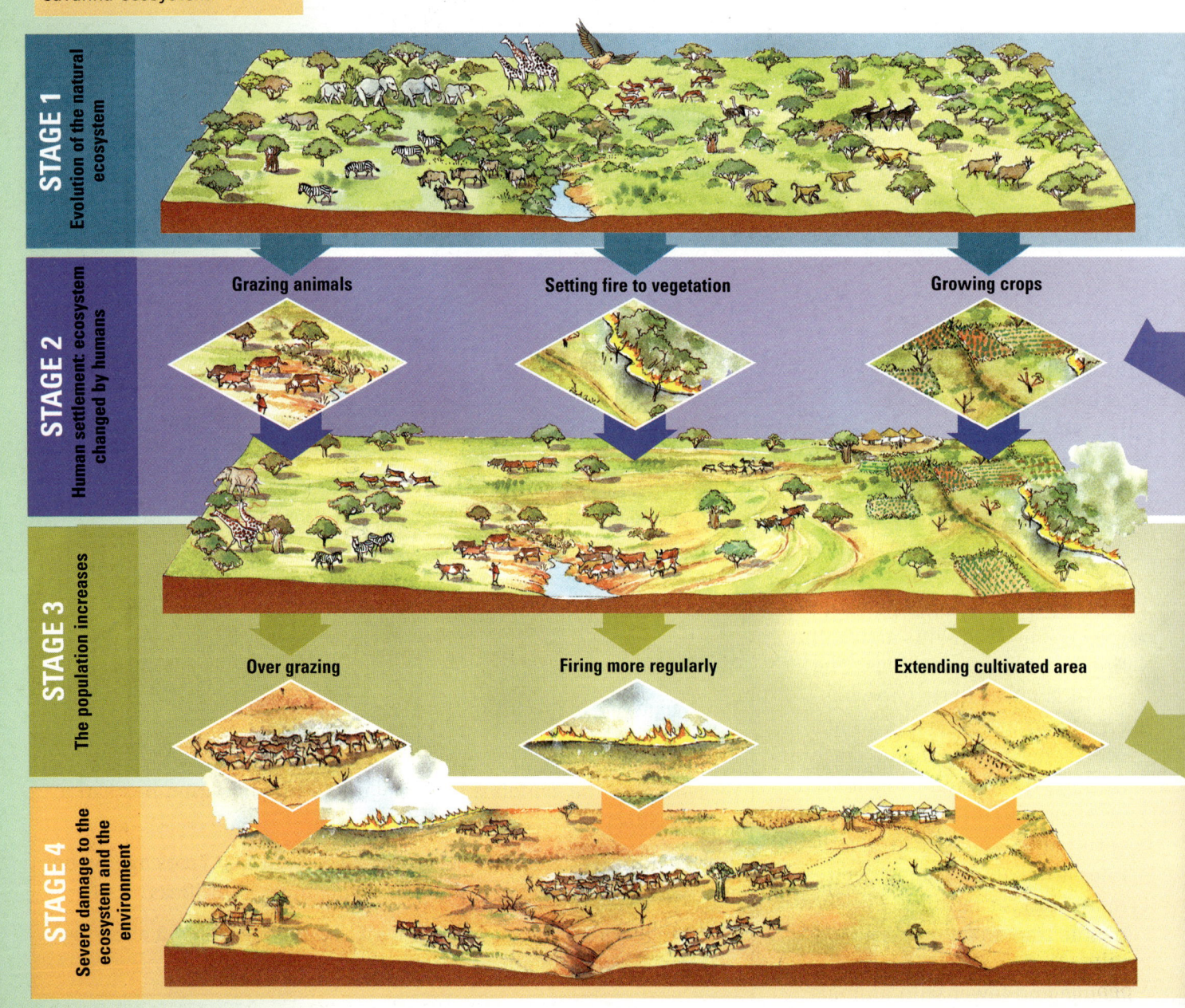

STAGE 1 — Evolution of the natural ecosystem

STAGE 2 — Human settlement: ecosystem changed by humans
- Grazing animals
- Setting fire to vegetation
- Growing crops

STAGE 3 — The population increases
- Over grazing
- Firing more regularly
- Extending cultivated area

STAGE 4 — Severe damage to the ecosystem and the environment

Ecosystems

Group Activity

Assume that a position between stages 2 and 3 shown in Source 1 has been reached. The challenge is to suggest strategies for preservation and conservation of the savanna ecosystem. Remember that you have two things to take into account:

- You are trying to conserve the savanna ecosystem with its plants and wild animals.
- The local people have to make a living. They are poor and they are desperate to improve their quality of life and standard of living.

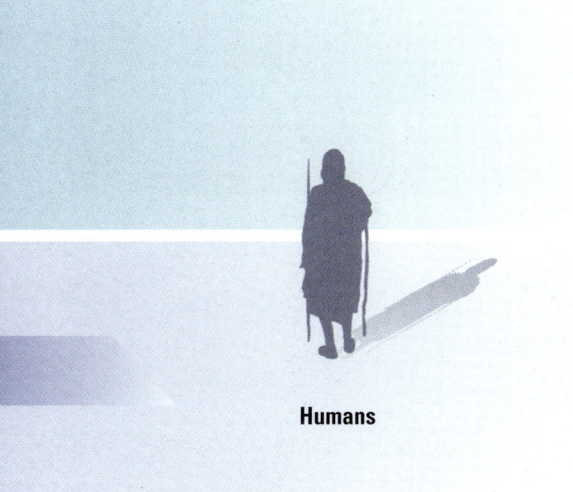

Humans

Population increase

Possible strategies

A Measures to reduce population growth

B Improved water supply – both water storage and laying pipes to take the water where it is needed

C Game control – confine the wild animals to reserves and parks

D Develop tourism – provide facilities for game viewing

What to do

a) As a group look at each strategy in turn – what could be done, what would be the good points and what would be the difficulties?

b) Decide upon what it would be best to do.

c) Draw a sketch to show what you would do. (Looking again at Source 3 on page 47 might help you.)

Summary

The vegetation element, which forms an important part of all ecosystems, is vital to life on earth. The many different climates have allowed great variety and diversity in plant life to develop. Modern farming and food supply depends upon growing plants and keeping animals which originally came from the world's natural ecosystems.

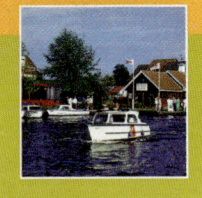

Managing environments

Source 1
Derwent Water, Cumbria

In this unit you will:
- learn about some special landscapes: the Norfolk Broads; the Alps; the tundra
- investigate why such landscapes need to be protected and managed
- find out how a reliable supply of fresh water is provided
- learn about the causes, effects and prevention of water pollution.

Look carefully at Source 1.
- What is 'special' about the landscape shown in the photograph?
- How might the actions of people damage the environment shown?
- What do you think is being done to protect the environment shown?
- How can areas of beautiful scenery be protected for the future?

Managing environments

National Parks

Some parts of the countryside in Britain have always been viewed as having especially beautiful scenery. As long ago as 1949, the government recognised the need to look after such areas. An Act of Parliament set up the ten **National Parks** in England and Wales (Source 2). Its aims were to:

- protect the special character of the landscape
- promote enjoyment by the public of open-air recreation
- control and protect traditional local activities.

Each National Park has a Planning Board to manage it.

Activity 1

Look carefully at Source 2.

a) Describe the location of National Parks in Great Britain. Use the points of the compass. An atlas map may also help you.

b) Compare Source 2 with a relief map of Great Britain. Comment on:

i) the connection between the location of the National Parks and relief

ii) the location of the National Parks compared with the main cities.

Most people (50% of the population) visit the countryside once a month, though not everyone lives near a National Park. Other parts of the countryside also have special status including: Areas of Outstanding Natural Beauty, Forest Parks, Nature Reserves and Country Parks. Do you have any of these special areas near where you live?

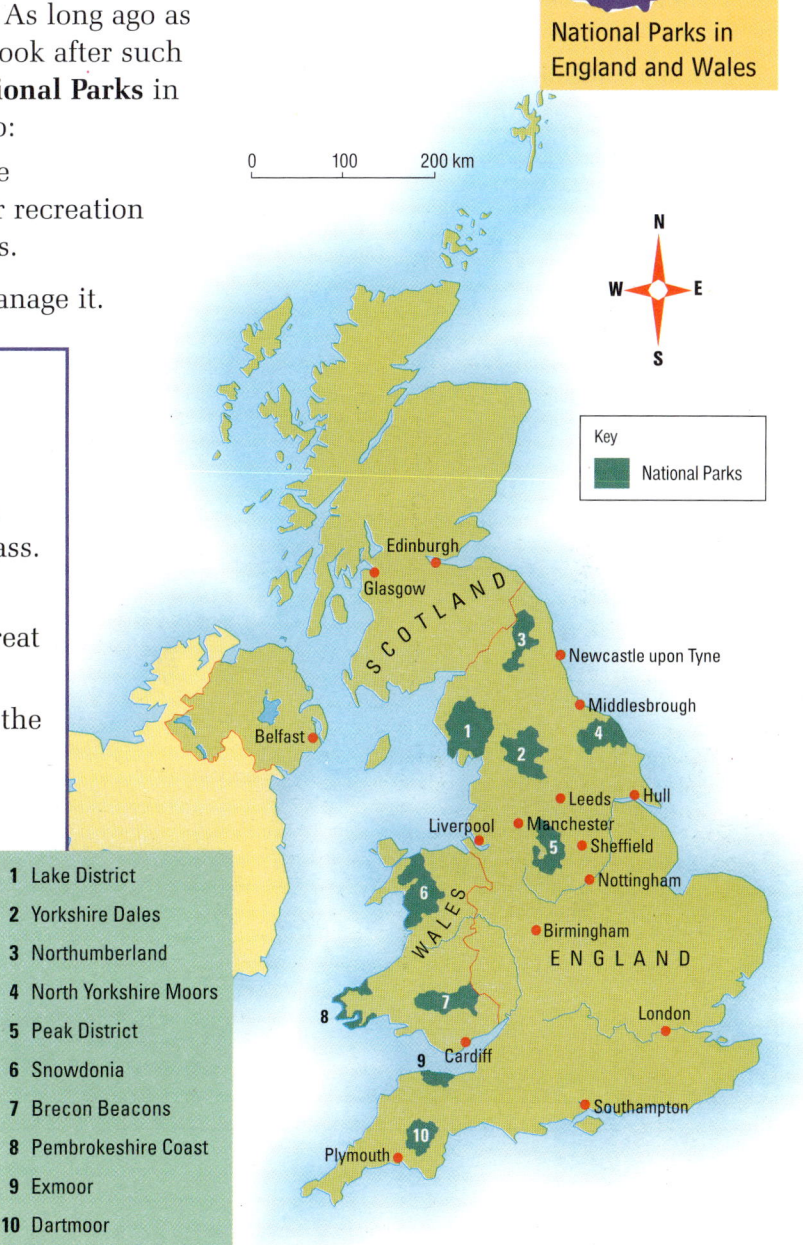

Source 2

National Parks in England and Wales

1 Lake District
2 Yorkshire Dales
3 Northumberland
4 North Yorkshire Moors
5 Peak District
6 Snowdonia
7 Brecon Beacons
8 Pembrokeshire Coast
9 Exmoor
10 Dartmoor

Activity 2

a) List three leisure activities which people enjoy in the countryside. Beside each one describe the type of scenery which is required for each activity.

b) Use Source 2 to calculate how far you live from the nearest National Park.

Group Activity

In small groups see if you can decide why the government thought that the National Parks would be viewed as having *great scenic attraction*. Bear in mind that eight out of every ten people in Great Britain live in a lowland urban area.

The changing British countryside

Over the last 50 years, methods of farming have changed a lot. These changes have altered the appearance of the landscape in many parts of lowland Britain, as Source 1 shows.

Source 1

The landscape in East Anglia in 1945 and 1995

Activity 1

a) Look at Source 1. Make a list of differences between the landscape in 1945 and in 1995. See how many you can find.

b) Copy the table (on the right) and place a tick in each row to show the correct answer.

c) Give reasons for your answers in the table.

	1945 landscape	1995 landscape
This landscape would produce more arable crops such as wheat, barley and oilseed rape.		
This landscape would provide more habitats for butterflies, birds and small mammals.		
This landscape would have the greatest number and variety of wild flowers.		
This landscape may suffer from soil erosion when there are strong winds.		

Managing environments

In recent years large companies, with no experience of farming, have bought up large areas of land and turned them into farms. They aim to make as much money as they can, by running them as businesses. Computers are used to keep detailed records of each field and to obtain up-to-date information on the prices of crops, feedstuffs and fertilisers. Accountants help to make decisions about what to plant in each field. These companies often grow, process, package and sell the food we eat and they make so much profit that they have turned farming into **agribusiness**.

Modern farming practice has changed the appearance of the countryside: hedgerows have been removed, pesticides are polluting the rivers and there is serious soil erosion. These changes have made people more aware about the damage being done by some modern farming methods. Gradually, farmers are being encouraged by the government and others, to take the **needs of the environment** into account.

The Countryside Commission runs a scheme called Countryside Stewardship which aims to make **conservation** a major part of farming practice. The scheme gives payments for changes in management practice that will conserve the landscape and its wildlife, improve access to the countryside and increase people's enjoyment of it. Source 2 shows some management measures for which payments are available. In 1988 the European Union (EU) began to make **set-aside payments** to farmers if they left some of their land unused, in order to reduce their farm output by up to 20 per cent. Trees are being planted on some of this land to create small woods.

Activity 2

a) Study Source 2, then list three ways in which the Countryside Stewardship scheme is changing the countryside.

b) What effect do you think these changes will have on the output (yields) of farmers?

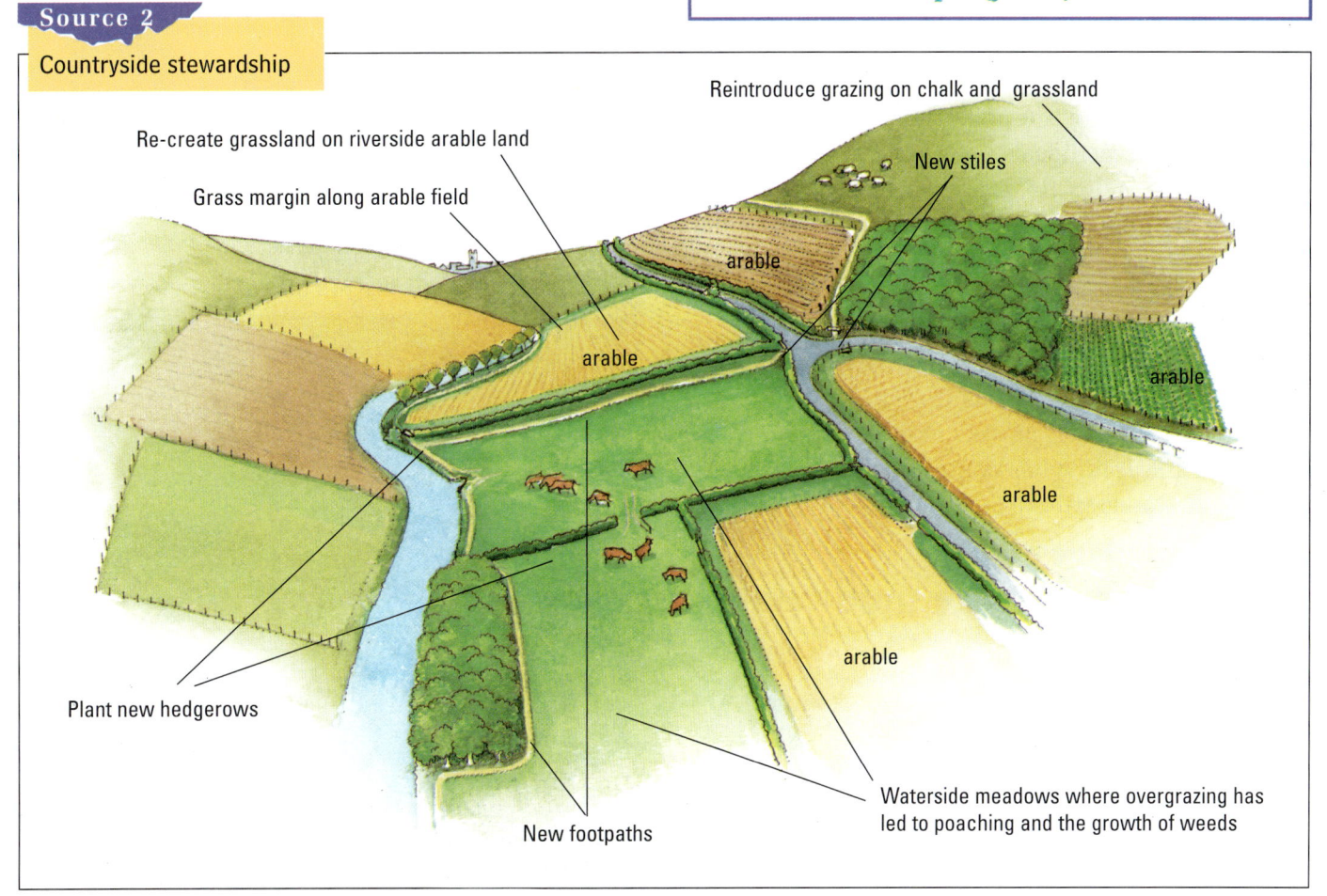

Source 2

Countryside stewardship

- Re-create grassland on riverside arable land
- Grass margin along arable field
- Reintroduce grazing on chalk and grassland
- New stiles
- Plant new hedgerows
- New footpaths
- Waterside meadows where overgrazing has led to poaching and the growth of weeds

53

The Norfolk Broads

The area known as the Norfolk Broads covers an area of 300 square kilometres in the valleys of the Rivers Bure, Ant, Thurne and Yare in Norfolk and the River Waveney on the Norfolk/Suffolk border. In contrast to the National Parks, it is a lowland area, located near the coast of East Anglia (see Source 1). There are rivers and open **broads**, or lakes, which are suitable for boats and have attracted many tourists and holidaymakers (see Source 2). The area also has woodlands, marshes and farmland, as well as towns with industry.

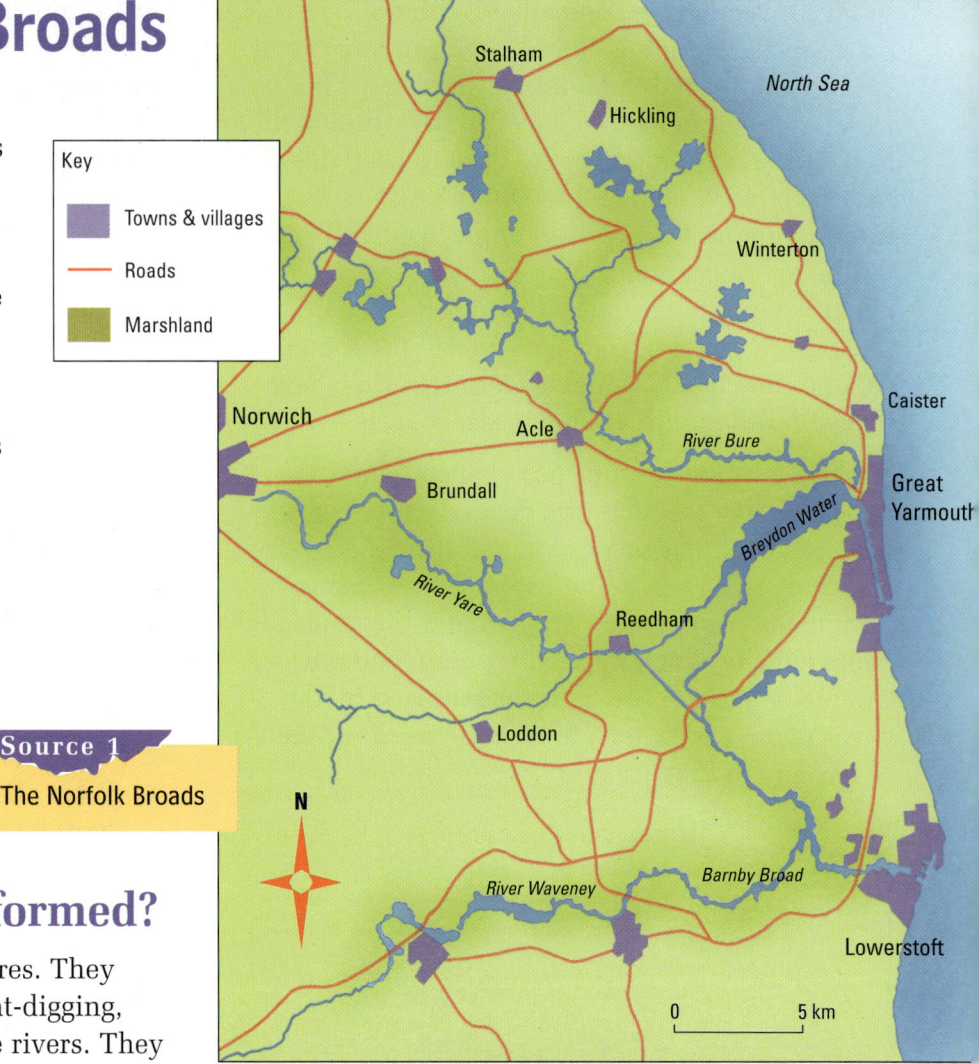

Source 1
The Norfolk Broads

How were the Broads formed?

The open broads are not natural features. They were formed in medieval times by peat-digging, mainly on the valley floors next to the rivers. They were dry then, but became flooded due to a gradual rise in sea level. Today the Broads give a unique landscape of outstanding natural beauty, rich in animal and plant life. However, the area must be carefully managed so that it can satisfy the demands made on it. In 1989 the Broads Authority was formed and given powers like those of a National Park. It now has control over planning, building and navigation.

What demands are made on the Broads?

The biggest demand is from leisure. Leisure has a useful impact on the environment, because it creates jobs and keeps people living and working in this rural area. However, the environment is being damaged especially by boats on the rivers and on the broads.

Source 2
Facilities for holidaymakers

Managing environments

Source 3
Demands made on the Broads

LEISURE

1 Sailing boats make little noise but motorboats do, and they go faster.

2 Traffic jams cause congestion in the smaller towns and villages.

FARMING

3 In the past, EU policy encouraged farmers to drain the marshland and grow cereals. This led to a loss of grazing land and wildlife habitats.

4 Cereals need fertilisers. Nitrates from the fertilisers are washed into the rivers and broads, polluting them.

TOWNS AND INDUSTRY

5 Towns put treated sewage into the rivers. However, it still contains phosphates.

6 Industries discharge effluent containing phosphates into rivers

Nitrates and phosphates

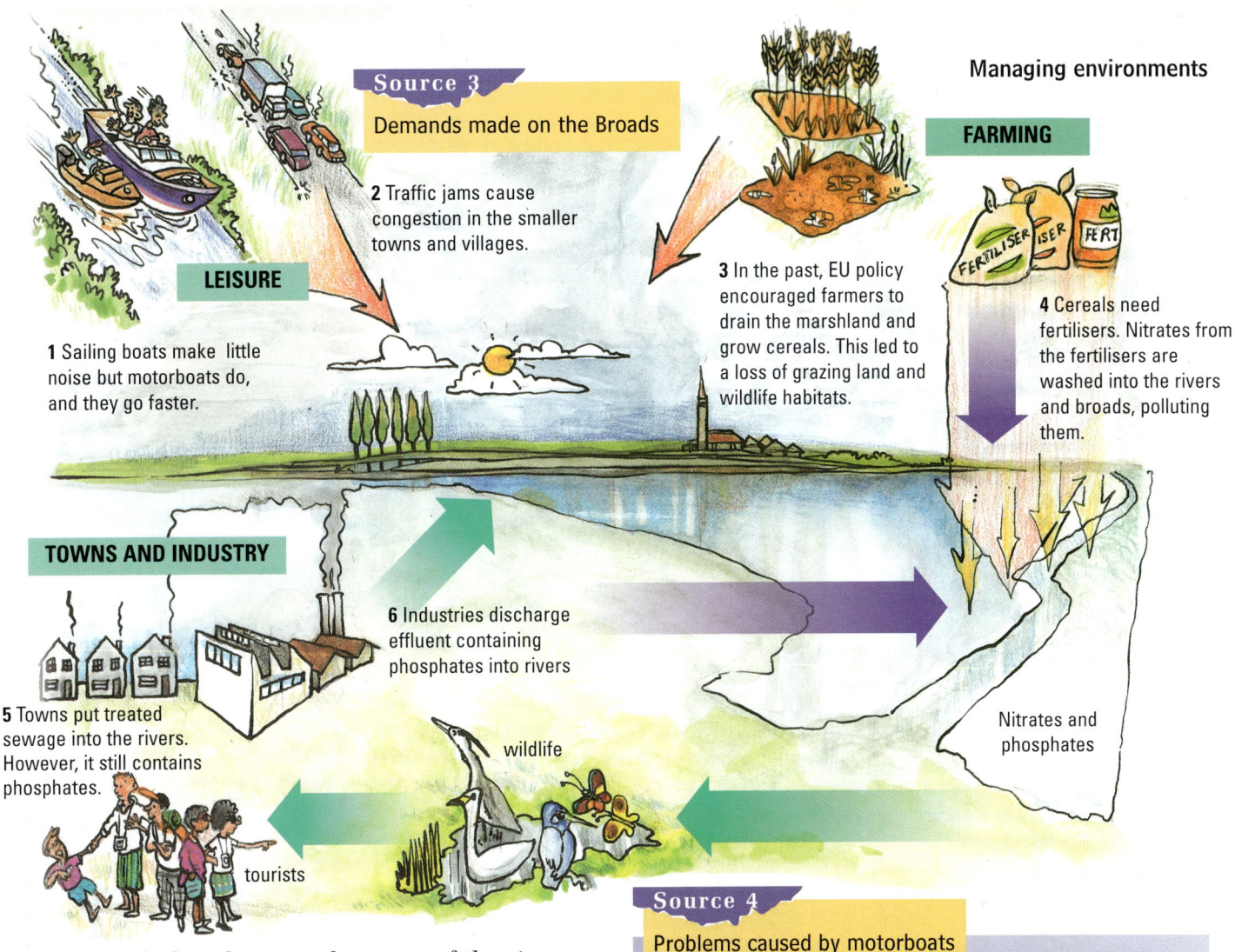

wildlife
tourists

Nitrates and phosphates in the water of the rivers and broads provide nutrients for tiny plants called algae. The algae grow and multiply, and turn the water cloudy making it difficult for other plants to grow. When the algae die, the bacteria which break them down use up all of the available oxygen in the water. This makes it difficult for other plants and animals to live.

Source 4
Problems caused by motorboats

1. bank erosion caused by the wash of boats going too fast
2. oil pollution
3. noise disturbance
4. congestion on the rivers
5. visual pollution
6. sewage effluent

BUT tourists provide jobs!

Activity 1

a) Think of all the jobs which tourism has brought to the area. Make a table with two columns and classify them into two groups:
   i) land-based activities
   ii) water-based activities.

b) Think of all the negative effects of tourism. Make a list of them. Which problems on your list were
   i) caused on land
   ii) caused on rivers and the broads?

Group Activity

Work in pairs for this activity. Imagine you and a partner have just taken over a company which hires out motorboats to tourists. You both want your customers to be more careful about the environment. Design a poster together to put up inside the boats to tell them about ways to use the boat carefully. Make your message positive, rather than full of 'don'ts'.

Managing Alpine environments

In the mountains of the French Alps, the traditional way of life was based on **pastoral farming**. Today this is only found in a few remote places in high valleys.

In the early twentieth century, the area suffered **rural depopulation** as people moved away to get better jobs in the cities. Recently, the rise of tourism, especially skiing, has led to an increase in population in many Alpine areas. This has had many effects, as Source 1 shows.

Source 1

An Alpine landscape before and after 1950

BEFORE 1950
- forested slopes
- traditional farming
- swift mountain streams

AFTER 1950

1 Development of hydro-electric power. Swift mountain streams have been dammed. Electricity has meant factories could be built in some of the valleys.

2 Development of tourism:

winter: ski slopes, lifts and cable cars – the clearing of slopes for ski runs and the building of apartments have led to increased runoff and decreased soil stability

summer: more summer visitors on paths and pastureland. Roads become congested. Hotels and other facilities are built.

Ecrins National Park

The French Alps have become a recreation area for the leisure-seeking urban population, with some farmers struggling to keep up the traditional way of life. To try and manage these competing demands, France has set up the Ecrins National Park (see Sources 2 and 3).

The Ecrins was made a National Park in 1973. It main aims are:
- to preserve natural culture – to understand and make understood the mountain way of life
- to develop scientific research – to map different types of plants and animals and to develop plans for conservation
- to welcome visitors – to provide information centres to educate people about the fragile nature of natural habitats and to respect mountain civilisation; to provide signposts, improve footpaths and make viewpoints
- to encourage local development – aid is given to attract and cater for tourists, buildings are restored and farmers are helped with traditional farming methods.

Source 2

Ecrins National Park

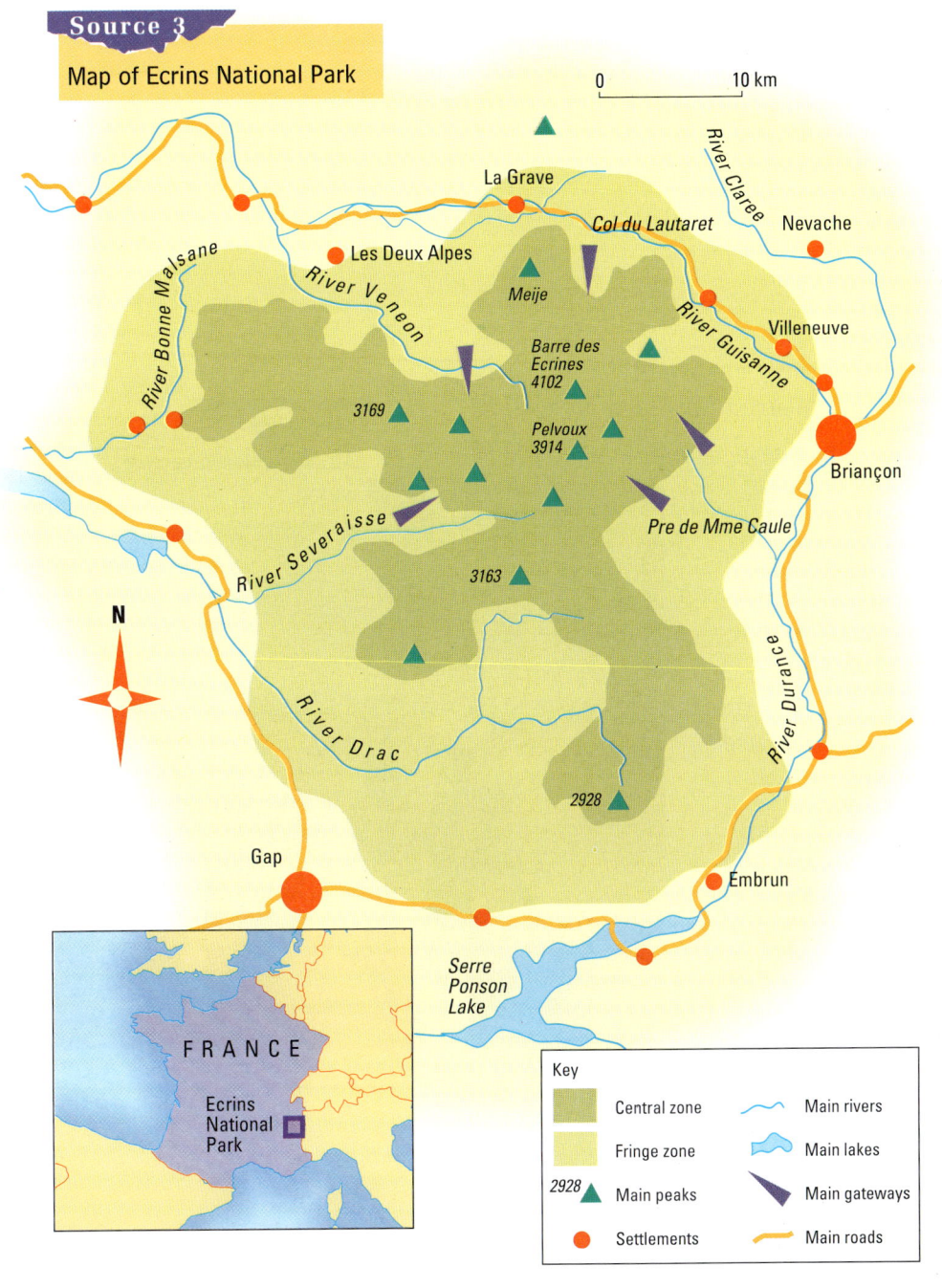

Managing environments

Source 3
Map of Ecrins National Park

Activity 1

Look at Source 3. Describe the relief of the National Park.

Protecting the Park

The Ecrins National Park has two zones:

- **fringe areas** – where some urban and tourist activities are allowed
- **central zone** – about 1/3 of the total area. This area is so high and the land is so rough that it can only be reached on foot. This area is easier to protect from mass tourism because it is so difficult to reach.

Source 4
The Ecrins National Park Code of Conduct

- Do not camp; bivouacing is allowed provided you are at least one hour's walk from a road or mountain hut.
- Do not bring your dogs. They disturb the wildlife and the sheep.
- Do not leave your rubbish. It litters the park and can injure others.
- Respect the flowers, berries, trees and rocks. Please do not pick them or take them away.
- Be careful with your cigarette. A thoughtless gesture can lead to fire.
- Do not make fires. They can cause disaster.
- Make no unecessary noise. The mountains will repay you with calm and tranquility.
- Camp only in the camp and caravan sites provided.
- Leave your gun behind. Here, every living species is protected.

Key: Central zone; Fringe zone; 2928 ▲ Main peaks; ● Settlements; Main rivers; Main lakes; Main gateways; Main roads

Activity 2

a) Look at Source 3. Draw a diagram to show the fringe areas and central zone of the park. Give it a title and labels to show how each part is protected.

b) Look at Source 4. Make a table with three columns to show:
   i) the symbols from the code of conduct
   ii) what types of conduct are expected
   iii) the **reasons** why each type of conduct is expected.

c) i) Why is each symbol shown on the palm of a large hand?
   ii) How well do you think the messages are shown?

Water management

In Britain we maintain a reliable water supply in three ways:
- by getting water directly from rivers
- by collecting water in reservoirs
- by pumping water from underground sources.

In England and Wales, the water companies must ensure that everyone has a reliable supply of clean water. There are strict European as well as British standards of water quality to be met.

Overall, Britain has enough rainfall in an average year to supply all the water that is required. It does not fall equally in all locations though. As a result, some areas do suffer shortages, and water companies rely on water being brought into their area by pipeline from other wetter regions. If there is a national shortage because of low rainfall across the whole country, then everyone must reduce their use of water.

In less economically developed countries (LEDCs), people are not so fortunate. Many people in rural areas have to collect water from rivers, ponds and wells, and then carry it back to their homes. Sometimes water must be carried over long distances (Source 1). The water is often polluted and dirty.

Source 1
African children carrying water

Activity 1

The table below shows the differences between the supply of water and the provision of drains and sewers in towns and in the country in less economically developed countries.

a) Draw a series of divided bar graphs to show the information in the table.

b) Why do you think that governments in developing countries seem to spend more money on supplying water and sanitation in towns than in the country?

c) In most parts of Britain, people pay 'water rates' for the water they use.

   i) Find out what your water rates are for your household per year.

   ii) Find out how your water company spends the money from your water rates.

Provision of water supply and sewers/drains in less economically developed countries (LEDCs)		
	% of population with water	% of population with sewers
towns (urban areas)	57% piped into house 20% by standpipe 23% have no piped water	25% of houses connected 50% have other arrangement 25% no facilities
countryside (rural areas)	29% have adequate supply	15% have adequate sewers
	71% have an inadequate supply	85% have inadequate provision

Managing environments

Water pollution: causes and effects

All over the world the water we drink which comes from rivers gives us cause for concern. Rivers are polluted in different ways in different parts of the world.

Source 2
Water pollution arguments

Developing country

Your stream contains untreated sewage and germs, which will cause liver damage, and make you very ill and encourage worms to grow inside your body.

But we have nowhere else to get our water from or bathe or wash our clothes. It takes me three hours to walk to the river and back. Often I feel tired and ill and so many of our babies die each year from diarrhoea.

Developed country

Lots of things end up in our rivers – the list seems endless: treated sewage, industrial chemicals, pesticides and nitrates from fertilisers, phosphates from detergents, even hot water from power stations! Are these things harmful?

Nitrates, phosphates and treated sewage damage life in our rivers by acting as fertilisers for plants and algae. Chemicals from industry can harm life in the river as well as the birds which eat fish. Hot water makes the river water warm so that it holds much less dissolved oxygen, and makes it difficult for river animals and plants to survive.

But what about the effect on our drinking water? I suppose you'll tell me that's why you're spending so much money adding even more chemicals to clean the water. No wonder our tap water tastes horrible.

Activity

Draw up a table like the one below:

	Developing country	Developed country
Causes of pollution		
Effects of pollution		
What results from the effects of pollution		

a) Look at Source 2. Use the information from it to fill in your table.

b) How would your life be different if you had a three-hour round trip each day to fetch the water your family needed from a river?

Group Activity

More and more people in Britain have water meters. This means that they pay for exactly what they use.

a) With a partner, discuss the good and bad points of water meters and water rates.

b) Design and produce a poster, advertising the good points of water meters.

Oil in the tundra

The **tundra** is a vast treeless area found mainly inside the Arctic Circle (Source 1). It extends across the northern part of North America and Asia. The soil is permanently frozen (permafrost), but in the short summer, the top metre thaws out into bogs and marshland with enough plant life to support insects, birds, foxes, hares and reindeer (Source 2).

The USA and CIS (former Soviet Union) need to extract the oil found in the fragile tundra environment to use in cities and industries further south.

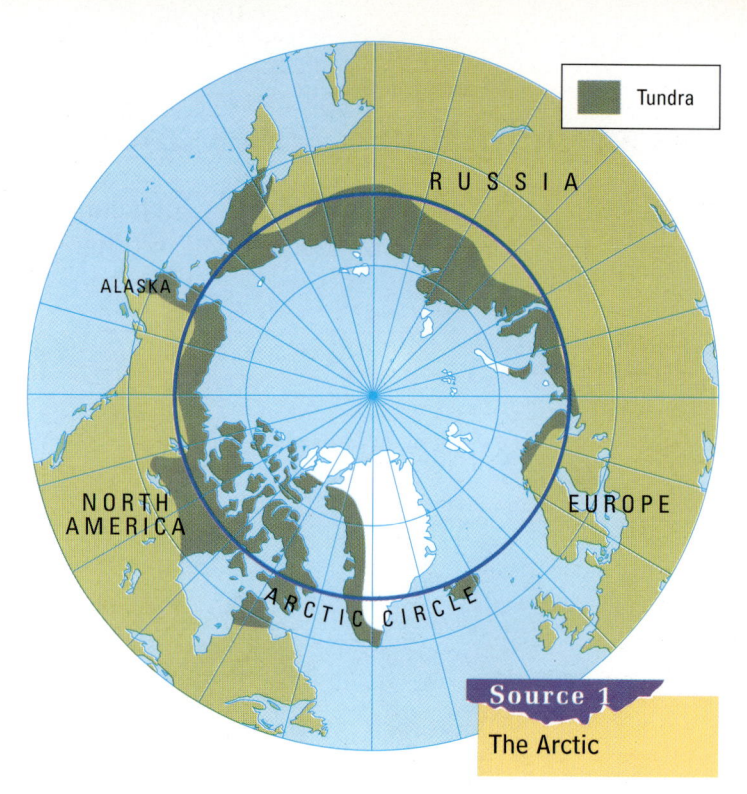

Oil from Alaska

The oil in Alaska is brought south across the tundra by pipeline. However, the tundra caused problems for the builders of the pipeline. The pipeline of hot oil rests on supports with thermal devices to keep the ground frozen - otherwise the pipeline would melt the permafrost forming a deep trench. To allow migrations of reindeer, the pipeline was raised 3 metres above the ground in some places – in others, it was buried in refrigerated and insulated trenches.

Conservationists saw Alaska as one of the last great wilderness areas of the world and wanted it to be protected and kept as natural as possible. But oil and mining companies needed to use the resources found in Alaska. A compromise was reached and the companies promised the highest standards of safety for the pipeline. There have been no oil spills on land in Alaska, but the Exxon Valdez oil tanker had a big spill in Prince William Sound in 1989.

Source 1 The Arctic

Source 2 Tundra in summer and winter

Activity 1

a) Use Source 1 to help you describe the location of the tundra regions.

b) Copy and complete the table below to show the difficulties of building the Trans-Alaskan pipeline through the tundra:

Problems of building an oil pipeline through a tundra area	How those problems were solved
Permafrost	
Seasonal migrations of reindeer	

c) Draw labelled diagrams to show the solutions to the building problems as detailed in your table.

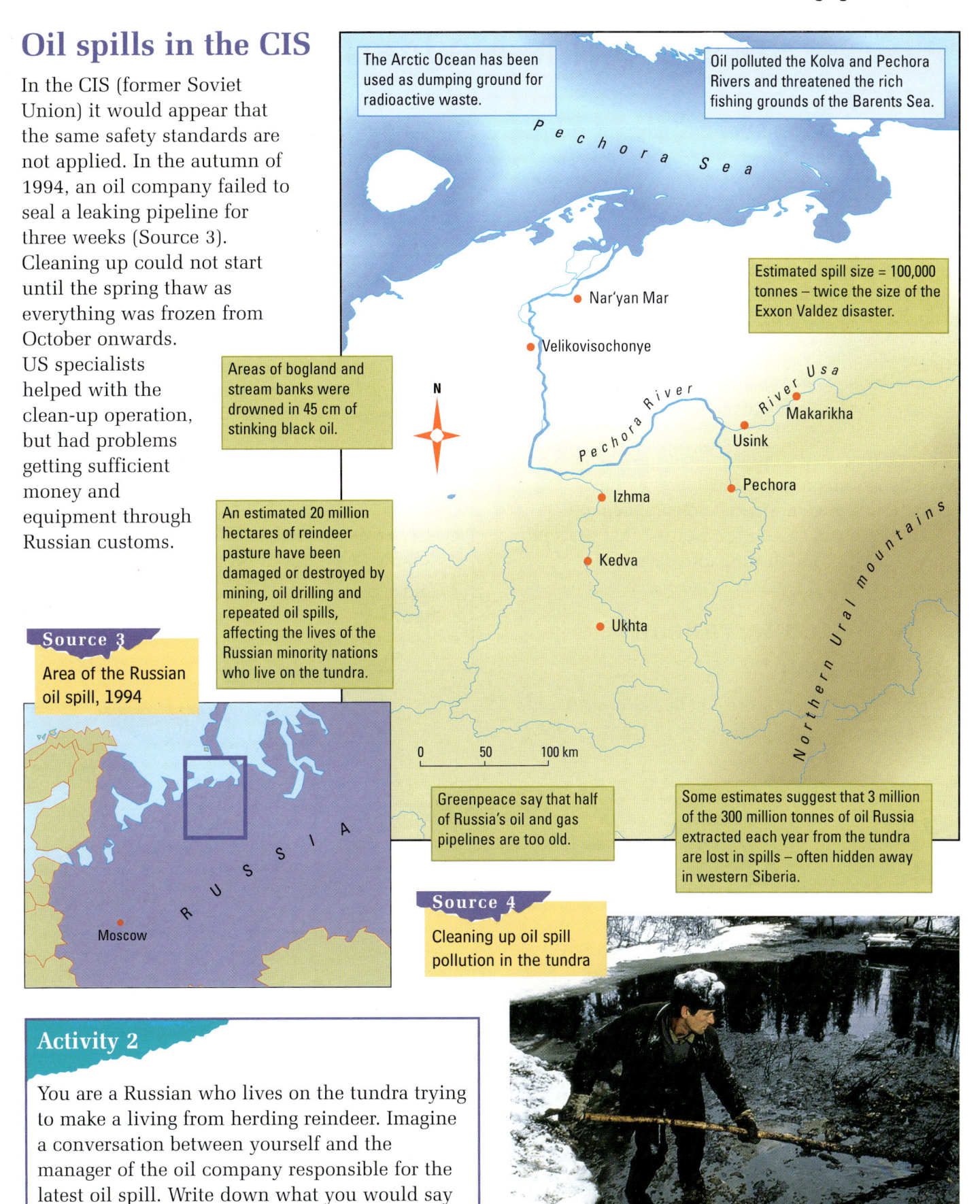

Managing environments

Oil spills in the CIS

In the CIS (former Soviet Union) it would appear that the same safety standards are not applied. In the autumn of 1994, an oil company failed to seal a leaking pipeline for three weeks (Source 3). Cleaning up could not start until the spring thaw as everything was frozen from October onwards. US specialists helped with the clean-up operation, but had problems getting sufficient money and equipment through Russian customs.

The Arctic Ocean has been used as dumping ground for radioactive waste.

Oil polluted the Kolva and Pechora Rivers and threatened the rich fishing grounds of the Barents Sea.

Estimated spill size = 100,000 tonnes – twice the size of the Exxon Valdez disaster.

Areas of bogland and stream banks were drowned in 45 cm of stinking black oil.

An estimated 20 million hectares of reindeer pasture have been damaged or destroyed by mining, oil drilling and repeated oil spills, affecting the lives of the Russian minority nations who live on the tundra.

Greenpeace say that half of Russia's oil and gas pipelines are too old.

Some estimates suggest that 3 million of the 300 million tonnes of oil Russia extracted each year from the tundra are lost in spills – often hidden away in western Siberia.

Source 3
Area of the Russian oil spill, 1994

Source 4
Cleaning up oil spill pollution in the tundra

Activity 2

You are a Russian who lives on the tundra trying to make a living from herding reindeer. Imagine a conversation between yourself and the manager of the oil company responsible for the latest oil spill. Write down what you would say to him and his possible replies.

Last Resort for the Mediterranean?

People have been changing the landscape around the Mediterranean Sea for over 2,000 years (Source 1). Trees have been cut down to build boats, and the slopes have been terraced to grow crops. Since 1950, the scale and pace of change has increased:

- many people have left rural areas to work in the cities and in the tourist industry
- there has been a flood of tourists to the coasts
- farming has become more modern, demanding fertilisers, more water and machinery
- many motorways have been built.

The Mediterranean environment has changed rapidly and major problems today include pollution, water shortages and rural depopulation. Spain, Italy and Greece are worried that parts of their countries are turning into deserts.

Future Mediterranean landscapes?

Can the Mediterranean region be better managed? Which of the future landscapes in Source 2 do we want to see?

Activity 1

a) Copy the table below.

b) Complete it by taking the viewpoint of each of the groups of people in turn, and giving a tick in the column of the future landscape you would most like to see.

	Traditional landscape	Desertified landscape	Managed landscape
Older people			
Younger people			
Tourists			
Local farmers			
The government			

c) Give reasons to explain your choices for the following groups of people:
- older people
- tourists
- local farmers.

Source 1
The Mediterranean

Key

Agriculture
- Arable land
- Irrigated land
- Fruits and vines
- Limit of olive growing

Environment
- Clean or slightly polluted
- Badly polluted
- Very badly polluted

Group Activity

Work in pairs.

a) Discuss your results for the above Activity with your partner.

b) Select a group of people from the table who chose the managed landscape. With your partner write a letter to your local government official which:

i) states which future Mediterranean Landscape you want to see, and

ii) explains what measures you think the government should take to make sure it happens.

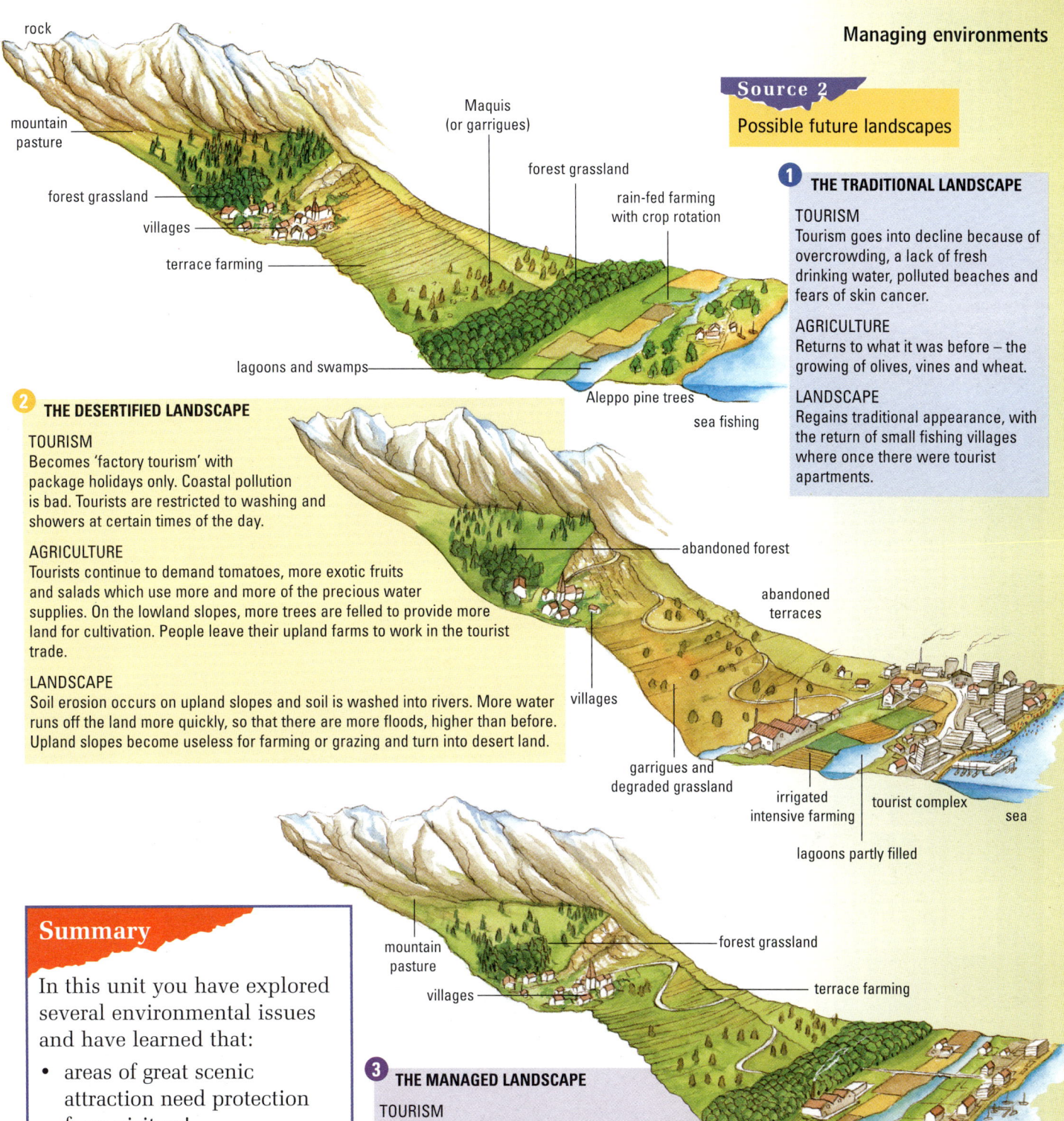

Managing environments

Source 2
Possible future landscapes

Labels on landscape 1: rock, mountain pasture, forest grassland, villages, terrace farming, Maquis (or garrigues), forest grassland, rain-fed farming with crop rotation, lagoons and swamps, Aleppo pine trees, sea fishing

① THE TRADITIONAL LANDSCAPE

TOURISM
Tourism goes into decline because of overcrowding, a lack of fresh drinking water, polluted beaches and fears of skin cancer.

AGRICULTURE
Returns to what it was before – the growing of olives, vines and wheat.

LANDSCAPE
Regains traditional appearance, with the return of small fishing villages where once there were tourist apartments.

② THE DESERTIFIED LANDSCAPE

TOURISM
Becomes 'factory tourism' with package holidays only. Coastal pollution is bad. Tourists are restricted to washing and showers at certain times of the day.

AGRICULTURE
Tourists continue to demand tomatoes, more exotic fruits and salads which use more and more of the precious water supplies. On the lowland slopes, more trees are felled to provide more land for cultivation. People leave their upland farms to work in the tourist trade.

LANDSCAPE
Soil erosion occurs on upland slopes and soil is washed into rivers. More water runs off the land more quickly, so that there are more floods, higher than before. Upland slopes become useless for farming or grazing and turn into desert land.

Labels on landscape 2: abandoned forest, abandoned terraces, villages, garrigues and degraded grassland, irrigated intensive farming, tourist complex, lagoons partly filled, sea

③ THE MANAGED LANDSCAPE

TOURISM
Present tourist areas are kept the same but the tourists are educated to become more aware of the water-supply problem. New developments are more expensive environment-friendly resorts. The EU gives grants to clean up pollution.

AGRICULTURE
Tourists' tastes are turned back to traditional foods which need less water to grow. Grants are available to farmers to replant maquis scrub to keep the soil in place. EU grants are available for environmentally sensitive areas. The farmers who own the land are given training to become 'environmental managers'.

LANDSCAPE
Soil erosion and desertification are slowed down and managed by more farmers who are paid to stay in rural areas.

Labels on landscape 3: mountain pasture, villages, forest grassland, terrace farming, sea

Summary

In this unit you have explored several environmental issues and have learned that:

- areas of great scenic attraction need protection from visitors!
- if people understand the need for environmental management, they will cooperate with environmental policies
- water pollution remains a global problem, but it means different things depending on where you live

Population

Source 1

A street in Tokyo, Japan

In this unit you will learn about:
- where people live and how crowded places are
- why people move from one place to another
- what happens to people who have moved and the places they have moved to.

Look at the photograph in Source 1 of a crowded street in Tokyo, Japan.

- What other places in the world are this crowded?
- What problems can arise from so many people?
- Do you know any places where no one lives at all?

Have you ever thought about what would happen if the world's population just kept growing and growing? How would we feed everyone? Where would people live?

Population

The challenge of population growth

At the moment there are about 5,607 million people in the world. It is estimated that by 2025 this will grow to over 8,000 million people. That means that the world's population is doubling in about 40 years.

Many people have different opinions as to what a population explosion would mean (Source 2). These opinions often depend on where the person lives and what their life style is like.

Source 2

Statements about population growth

Many developing countries are not heavily populated. Developed countries have more people but they can cope.

The question is, who controls the world's resources and who uses most of them?

The population crisis should be solved by massive programmes of birth control.

The world's population is growing too fast.

The reasons why many people choose to have a lot of children is because they are poor – not the other way around.

The South is overpopulated and it doesn't have the resources to cope.

If people had fewer children they would be wealthier.

Source 3

Different life styles – different opinions?

Activity 1

a) Make a table like the one below:

Agree	Disagree

In pairs, decide in which column you think the statements in Source 2 should go. Write them in.

b) Draw a sketch of each of the two photographs in Source 3. Around the outside of each sketch write down the statements from Source 2 that you think that each person might have said.

Population growth

Population numbers are constantly changing. As more babies are born and surviving, and people are dying at an older age, the number of people who are alive is increasing. We call this population growth. The population **growth rate** measures how quickly or slowly the population numbers change.

The number of babies born per thousand people is called the **birth rate**, and the number of people who die (per 1,000 people) is called the **death rate**. Therefore, if 40 babies are born for every 1,000 people we can say that the birth rate is 40 per thousand. When the birth rate is greater than the death rate, this is called **natural increase**.

The rate of population growth can also change when people move in or out of an area. This is called **migration**. When people move into an area this is called **immigration**, and when people move out of an area, this is called **emigration** (Source 1).

Over the last 2,000 years, all these aspects of population change have led to a huge increase in the world's population as source 2 shows.

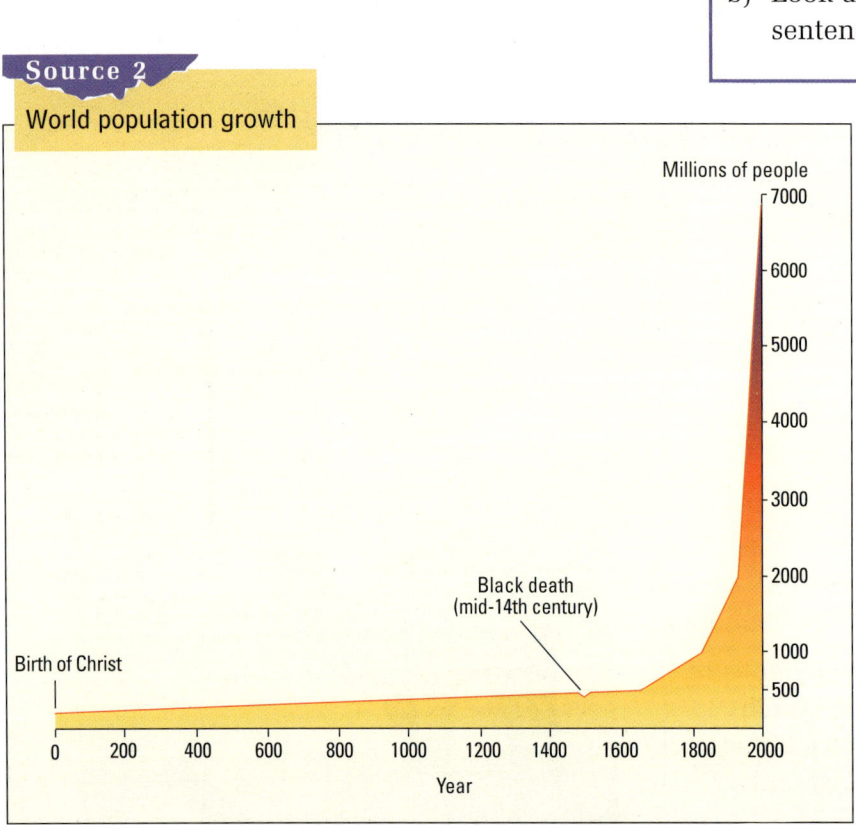

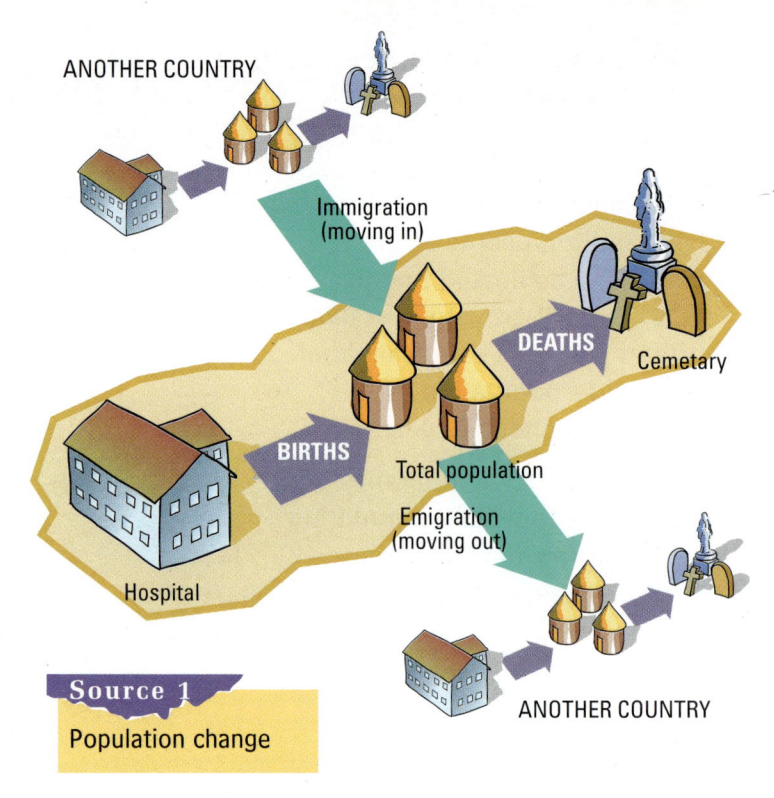

Source 1
Population change

Source 2
World population growth

Activity 1

a) Look at the words in heavy type. Write down in your own words what they mean.

b) Look at Source 1. Copy and complete these sentences:

i) If there are more births than deaths population growth will _____ .

(ii) If there are more deaths than births, population growth will _____ .

(iii) If the births and deaths remain the same, but people migrate into the area, the population growth will _____ .

(iv) If the births and deaths remain the same, but people move out of the area, the population growth will _____ .

c) Now make up some more sentences like the ones above and test your neighbour.

Population

Some areas of the world have a growing population, whilst others have a stable or decreasing population. Source 3 shows how the total number of people in each country is changing.

Source 2 shows how global population has increased over the last 2000 years. Rapid increase has only occurred in the last 400 years. This rapid increase is sometimes called the **population explosion**. There are a number of reasons for this:

- better medical knowledge and care mean people die older and more babies live for longer
- the decline in famine, war and disease
- the changes in agriculture and industry
- better sanitation and hygiene
- better nutrition.

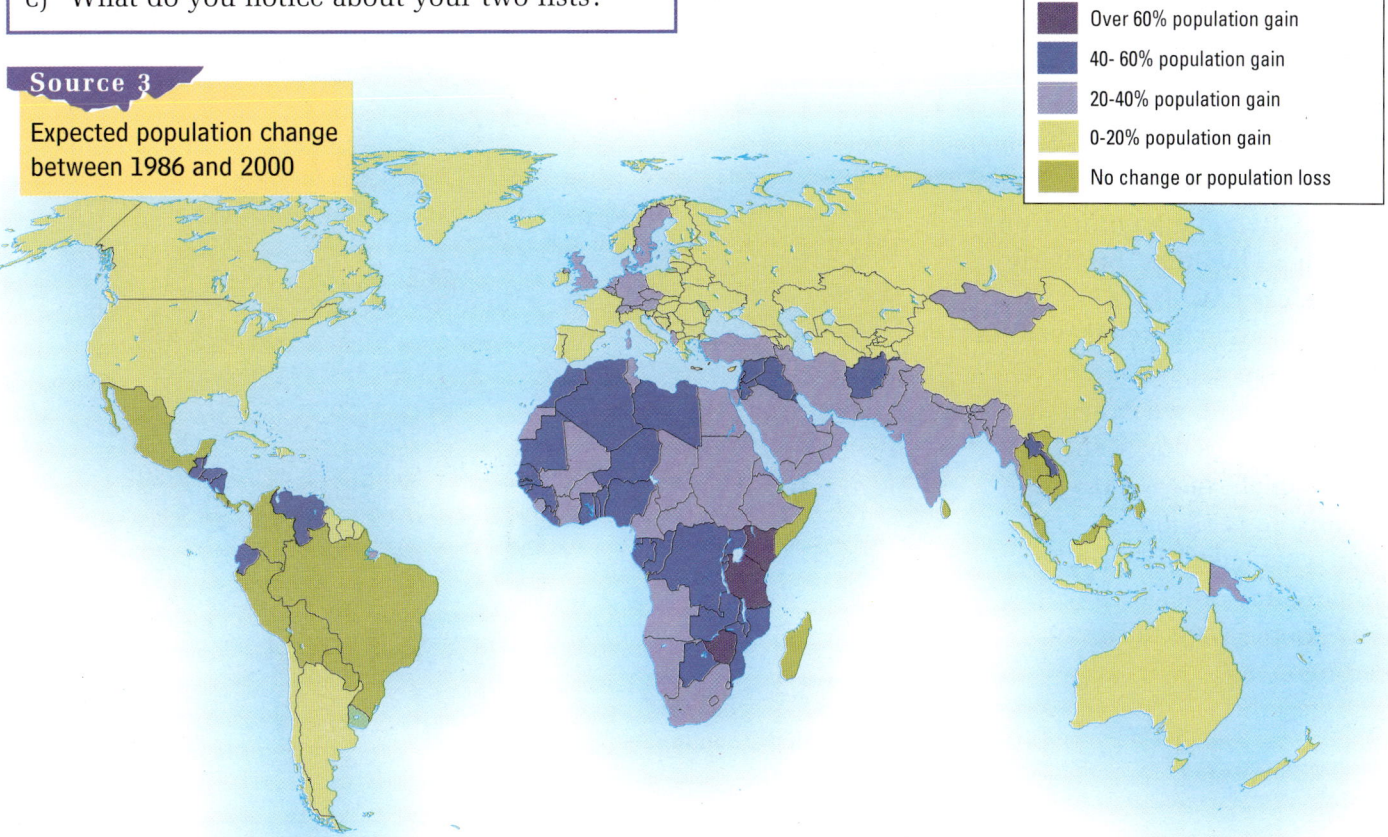

Activity 2

a) Look at Source 3. Using an atlas, list five countries with a decreasing or stable population.

b) List five countries with a high population growth.

c) What do you notice about your two lists?

Source 3

Expected population change between 1986 and 2000

Key
- Over 60% population gain
- 40-60% population gain
- 20-40% population gain
- 0-20% population gain
- No change or population loss

Activity 3

a) Using the words below, describe how global population has changed:

increased	death rate	agriculture
medicine	birth rate	decreased
nutrition		hygiene

b) Using the information on this page, write an introduction to a magazine article explaining why the world's population has 'exploded'. Suggest how you think that population may change in the future.

How are we spread out?

It is estimated that 80 per cent of the world's population live in cities. However, only 20 per cent of the land is taken up with cities. That means that there are areas of the world where very few people live.

Population can change on many scales: e.g. globally, within a continent or country, and on a local level. **Population density** is a measure of how crowded a place is.

Some parts of the world have a lot of people living in them. This is called high population density. Where there are few people living in an area, this is called low population density. The map in Source 1 shows how people are spread out in the UK.

People live in different areas for different reasons. Some areas are more attractive than others, and have more facilities. Similarly some areas have more employment and people want to live there to get better jobs. On the other hand, when an industry closes down, then people might move away from the area to get a job somewhere else. Can you think of any other reasons why people want to live in certain areas?

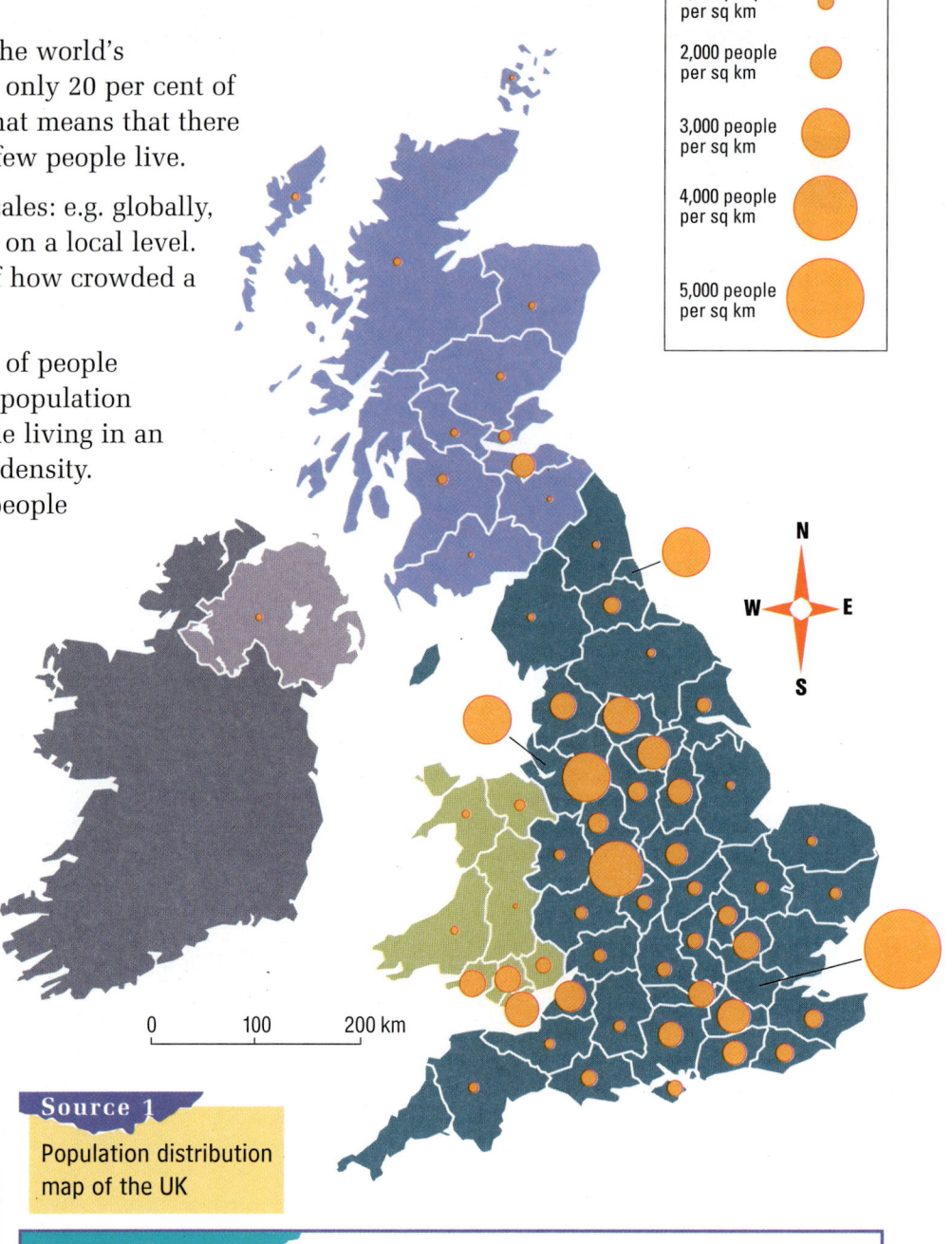

Key
- 1,000 people per sq km
- 2,000 people per sq km
- 3,000 people per sq km
- 4,000 people per sq km
- 5,000 people per sq km

Source 1
Population distribution map of the UK

Word list
birth rate
death rate
family planning schemes
growth rate
migration
population distribution
population density
population explosion
resources

Activity

a) Name 5 counties in Source 1 where there is high population density. Use your atlas to help you.

b) Name 5 counties where there is low population density.

c) In pairs, describe the pattern that you can see. (Hint: what do you notice about where the places with a high population density are? Use an atlas for more clues!) Can you find out reasons for this pattern?

There are many ways that we can show where people live on a map. On the map in Source 1, different sizes of dots have been used to show different population densities. This type of map is called a **dot distribution map**. We can also use different colours to show the same thing, like the map on page 67 and the map below. These are called a **choropleth maps**.

Source 2

Population density of countries in Europe

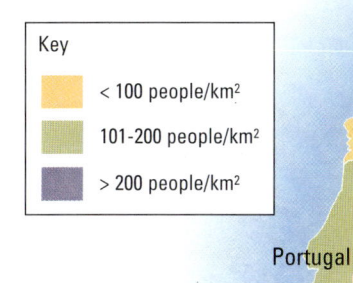

Key
- < 100 people/km^2
- 101–200 people/km^2
- > 200 people/km^2

Source 3

San Gimignano, Tuscany. Italy

Activity 2

a) Using a blank map of Europe and Source 2, decide on the best way to show the population distribution of Europe. (Clue: choose either the dot distribution method, or the colour shading method to fill in your blank map.)

b) Write a paragraph explaining what patterns the map shows.

Why do people move?

People move for many reasons. Some people move to a different city for work, some to a better home. People also move to different places: a neighbouring town, a different area or even a new country.

Maria used to live in rural Peru but recently moved to Lima. She moved because her family were very poor in the rural area and they needed her to get work in the city, so that she could send them money. Maria explains how she felt about moving in Source 1.

Activity 1

a) How many reasons can you think of for people moving?

b) What does it feel like to move?

Source 1
Maria Vargos

> We were very happy in our village. We all worked hard on our farm and produced enough food for the whole family. Unfortunately, a large company has bought our land. We have little left and it is not enough to feed the family.

> My mother and father are too old to move and have my younger brothers and sisters to look after. So they sent me and my brother to Lima to get work so we can send money home.

> We arrived in Lima and had never been to the city before. Neither of us knew anyone but we were both excited at the prospect of getting a job and somewhere to live. It certainly costs more to live here.

> Lima has so much more – cinemas, shops, big houses and buses. The only problem has been trying to find a job here. We can both read a bit but not a lot – this makes it difficult for us to get work. When we earn more money we are going to go to classes to learn to read better – we could never have done that at home.

We can put these reasons for moving into two categories: things that push people away from a place, and things that pull them somewhere else. These are called **push–pull factors** (Source 2). This is because urban areas like Lima 'pull' people towards them like a magnet (**urban pull**) and rural areas 'push' them away (**rural push**).

Population

Source 2
Push–pull factors

Rural push
- Unemployment
- Poor education
- Few medical facilities
- Difficult lifestyle

Urbal pull
- More jobs
- Better education
- Better medical facilities
- More services/amenities

Activity 2

a) In pairs, read what Maria has to say. Make a table with two columns headed 'Push' and 'Pull'. Write out her reasons under the appropriate column.

b) In a different colour add some of your own.

Sometimes when people have moved to an area they can be disappointed that it doesn't live up to what was expected. Maria and her brother hoped to be able to get a job in Lima but found that it was not as easy as they expected. When people move into a place they often have to take what housing they can find and this is often the cheapest and most run-down (Source 3).

Activity 3

a) In pairs, make your own push–pull diagram showing why people are moving out of UK cities.

b) Imagine you have just moved to the area in the picture from Peru in Source 1. Write a letter to a friend describing why you moved and what your new area is like, and how you feel about living there.

Source 3
Low quality housing

Urban pull and rural push doesn't just happen in developing countries like Peru. In the nineteenth century in the UK, farmers found it difficult to support their families and so many people moved to cities to get jobs in the new factories. The new industries that were growing then included iron and steel and coal mining. These industries needed lots of people to work in them and large cities grew up providing homes for the people that got jobs in the factories. Examples of these cities include: Glasgow, Newcastle, Manchester.

Now the trend has reversed in the UK, and people are looking for excuses to move out of the polluted, crowded cities to quiet rural areas. The increase in technology means that with phones, faxes and computers people no longer need to be in a city to work in hi-tech industries.

Is there a population challenge?

The main reason for the rising population figures is not that people are having large families. It is because death rates are falling, and so more people are living for longer. Governments tend to blame developing countries for population increase because people in these countries generally have larger families. Shanti from Bangladesh explains why in Source 1.

Why have a large family?

Activity 1

a) Using Source 1, make a list of reasons why people have large families.

b) Rank the reasons in terms of which you think is the most important.

Speech bubbles in Source 1:

- It is important as a woman to have children.
- I came from a large family and I want a large family. I love children and a home isn't a home without lots of children.
- I would like to educate my children to go to university so that they can get jobs to support me and be happy. But education is too expensive.
- Lots of children around here die when they are very young. If I have lots of children then more of them will survive.
- I need children to look after me when I'm old and ill. My children also work in the fields, on my own I couldn't produce enough food.

Source 1 Views on family size

It is argued that, despite these reasons, if women were given the choice they would choose to have smaller families. For Shanti to have a smaller family, she would need better medical care, so that all of her children would live, and better technology, so that she needed fewer people to work the farm. More children also means more mouths to feed. A better standard of living would mean there was less reason to have a large family.

Large families were once very common in the UK. But now people are choosing to have fewer children. With better family planning, and more people in full-time work, many couples have decided that they prefer smaller families.

Source 2 gives a list of reasons from a survey in which people were asked why they didn't want a large family.

Activity 2

Write a short magazine interview with a young professional couple. You are asking them why they have decided to have a small family.

Population

Population projections

We can estimate how much a population will grow, by looking at the structure of the population. We do this by looking at **population pyramids** (Source 3). A population pyramid shows us how many males and females there are in a country at different age groups. From this we can see how the population might change in the future. For instance, if there are a lot of people around 20–30 years old, it is likely that they will have lots of children and there will be a 'baby boom', meaning an increase in population. However, if there are lots of elderly people and few younger people, we can estimate that in the future the older people will die and there will not be enough babies to replace them. Therefore the total population will decrease soon. This does not tell us the whole picture, because having a large family also depends on the standard of living and religious beliefs.

Activity 3

a) Look at Source 3. Describe the population of each pyramid.

b) What differences are there between the pyramids?

c) Make a prediction about what will happen in the future for each country (i.e. will the population grow or decline?).

Source 2
Reasons for not having a large family

I'd rather have two children that I can give all my time and energy to than feel that I'm struggling with lots.

I like my life style as it is – I don't want children to change that – I don't want to stop going out!

We don't have the space for any more children – we'd have to move house.

We both have full-time jobs – any more children and one of us would have to give up work. Where would the money come from?

Source 3
Population pyramids

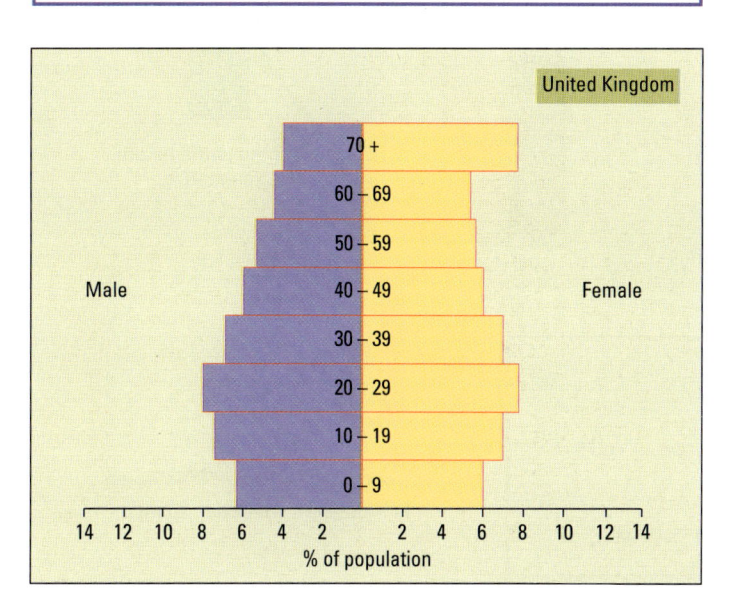

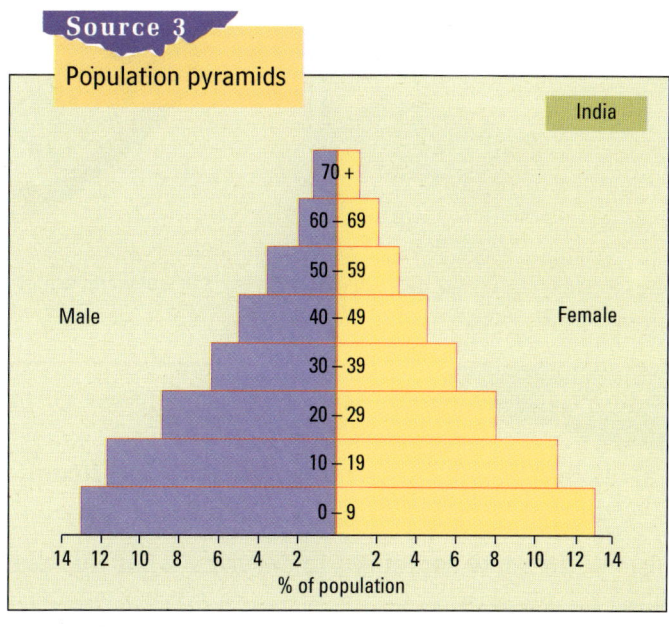

United Kingdom

India

73

Resources and population

The main challenge of population growth is the problem of having to feed a large and growing world population. Can the earth grow enough food?

Not everyone gets the same amount of food. The average American eats 40 times as much as the average Indian. Our supermarket shelves are usually well stocked (Source 1) but do we have enough food for everyone?

Source 1
People shopping in a supermarket

Source 2
Resources statistics

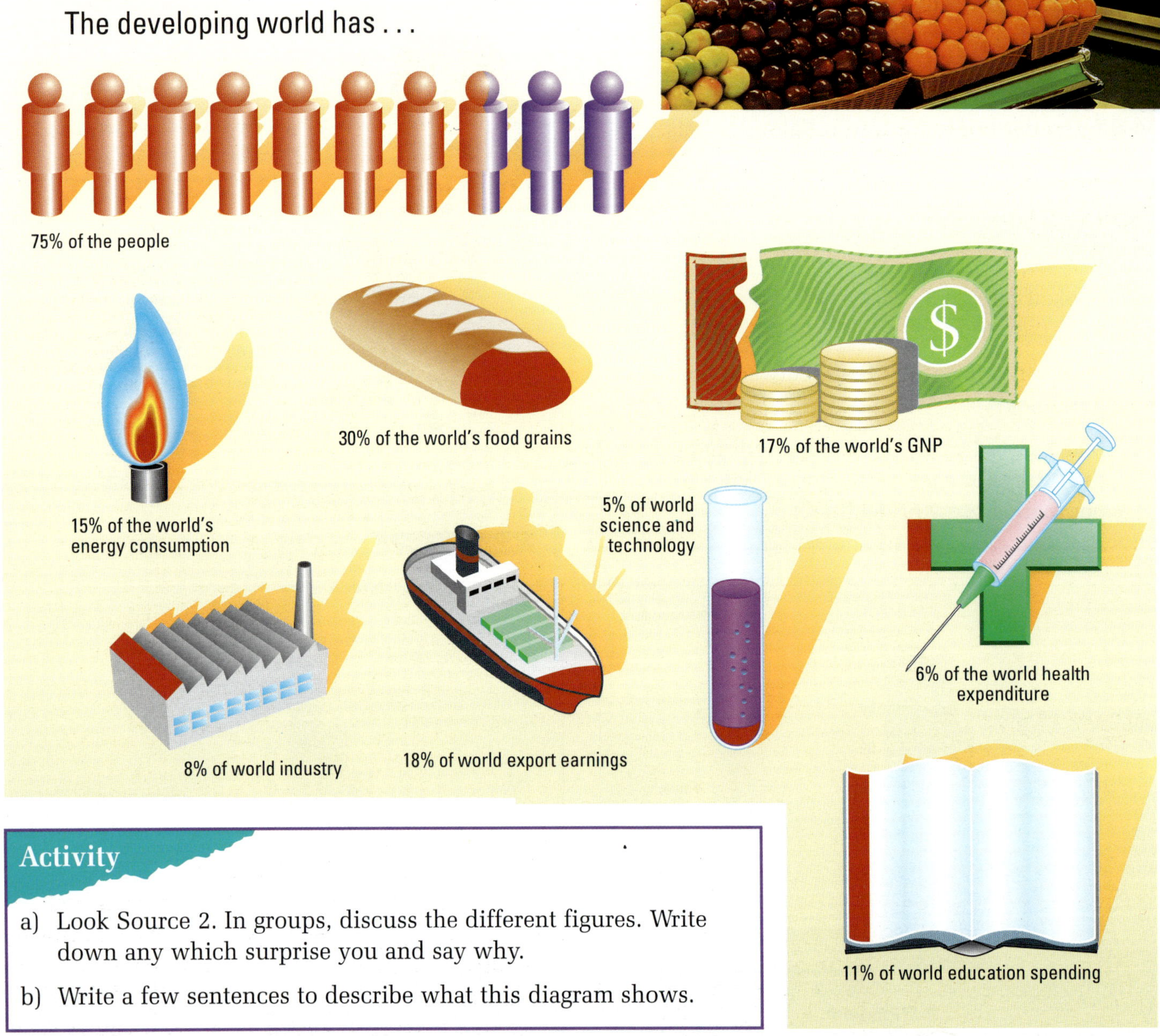

The developing world has . . .

75% of the people

15% of the world's energy consumption

30% of the world's food grains

17% of the world's GNP

8% of world industry

18% of world export earnings

5% of world science and technology

6% of the world health expenditure

11% of world education spending

Activity

a) Look Source 2. In groups, discuss the different figures. Write down any which surprise you and why.

b) Write a few sentences to describe what this diagram shows.

Population

Food is not the only resource that people need. There are two main types of resources. **Natural resources** are things like food, water, wood, gold and trees. People need some of these things to live. Natural resources are sometimes made into other items. These are called **manufactured resources**, and include cars, televisions and washing machines. Both types of resources are unequally spread across the world. If you live in a richer, more developed country you will have more access to manufactured resources.

Group Activity

Work in groups for this activity.

a) In pairs, make a list of natural and manufactured resources. Try to think of more than 10 of each.

b) Look at the cartoons in Source 3. Match each cartoon with a sentence from the list below.

c) Give a reason why you put them together.

d) Look at Source 4. Explain what the cartoon is trying to say.

e) So, is it a problem of resource distribution? Explain your answer.

- The developed world does not understand the real situation in the developing world.
- The developed and developing worlds should work together to produce a better world for all.
- Exploitation is starving the developing world.

Source 3
The developed and developing worlds

Source 4
North and south

Some people argue that resource allocation is the biggest factor in the population explosion. Resources are unequally distributed throughout the world. The real challenge is whether to reduce the consumption of resources in developed countries or to increase the availability of those resources in economically developing countries.

Managing population change

Most governments are aware of the potential problems of uncontrolled population growth. Many have already introduced policies to restrict population growth. China has a famous 'One Child Policy' where people are offered financial incentives if they only have one child, and there are heavy penalties if they have more than one (see Source 1). Not all policies are this strict.

India introduced a population policy in 1952 to make economic and social development easier. After a large survey of what people wanted and were doing, they realised that although people sometimes did not want any more children their knowledge of **contraception** was not good enough. The government therefore introduced **family-planning schemes** to teach people how to plan their families, so that they could control the size and timing of their family (Source 2).

Source 1
One Child Policy

The government of China believed that the problems of feeding, clothing, housing, educating and employing the population could all to be traced to a common cause – too many people. Their solution was to produce fewer people, so they introduced the single-child policy.

To try to persuade people to follow the one-child policy, the country adopted a system of economic rewards and penalties. Parents who limited their family to one child were given a five to ten per cent salary bonus. In addition, to their salary bonus, parents of only one child would also get better housing and medical care. The single child received priority in education and employment.

Similarly, those who had more than one child would find themselves disadvantaged in the same ways. Pressure would be exerted to have second pregnancies aborted: in 1983 14 million abortions were performed.

Source 3
Population policy in Thailand: initiatives from the government

Thailand	1969	1991
Population	26.4 million	58.8 million
Population growth	3% per year	1.3% per year
GNP per head	US$ 110	US$ 1220

Nationwide family-planning programme:
- freely available contraception
- family-planning clinics even in rural areas
- women trained to give correct contraception to others

1980s Mass-media campaign to encourage use of contraception

1990s People using contraception now risen from 14.7% to 68% in 20 years

Source 2
A family in India

Population

Activity 1

a) Using Source 3, draw a timeline showing the development of the population policy in Thailand.

b) What were the main points of the population policy in Thailand?

c) How did the government make sure people knew about contraception?

d) If you were a person living in Thailand or China, how would you feel about being told how many children you should have? Write a diary extract.

e) Using the table of population statistics in Source 3, write a short newspaper report saying how successful the policy has been in Thailand, and compare it to the population policies of China and India.

There are many other ways of slowing population growth. Source 4 shows a few ideas.

Activity 2

a) Rank the factors in Source 4, according to which you think is the most important for slowing down population growth.

b) If you had to make a population policy, which ideas from Source 4 would you include and why?

c) Write a letter to the government, setting out your ideas, how they would be carried out, and why they are good ideas.

d) Your population policy has been accepted. Make a poster that could introduce the policy and its benefits to the country.

Most countries have their own population policy now. Different policies have focused on contraception, or financial incentives to have few children. Governments are now realising that the best way to stop people having children is to increase their standard of living. The more money people have, the smaller their families tend to be.

Source 4
Some of the factors contributing to slower population growth rates

MORE EQUALITY FOR WOMEN

To provide educational and employment opportunities so that women have choices beyond childbearing.

BETTER FOOD AND HEALTH

To make sure that children survive a good supply of nutrients, immunisation against major disease, and good health care can be important.

APPROPRIATE TECHNOLOGY

Can take some of the drudgery out of farm work and lessen the need to have large families which provide labour on the land.

SOCIAL SECURITY

Pensions and sick pay take away the need to have children as an insurance policy.

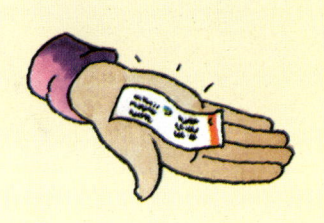

EDUCATION

To provide literacy and extend education. People with more education tend to marry later, have better jobs and smaller families.

FAMILY-PLANNING INFORMATION & SERVICE

To help people to have only the children they want and can care for.

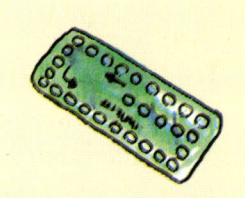

Rising to the challenge

Can the world continue to support an ever growing number of people? Governments have become so worried about this question that in 1994 a World Population Summit was held in Cairo (Sources 1 and 2) to debate the issues. Some people think that the growing population could lead to famine, war and the destruction of the global ecosystem.

Source 1

Cairo

Source 2

The 1994 Population Summit

Group Activity

You are going to take part in your own Population Summit. Working in groups of five, you must each choose a role, discuss it and make up a speech using the information here and what you have learnt in this unit. You will be asked to deliver your speech and then answer questions on it. It would be useful if you discuss what your group thinks with another group who have similar opinions. Eventually the Summit can decide on appropriate measures for the whole world to take.

Chairperson

You have been asked to chair this meeting. You are not allowed to take sides, but you must listen carefully to everyone and make sure that they all get a fair say. At the end you can discuss which arguments were the most convincing and why.

Population

Religions

You represent the Catholic Church. You believe that child birth is God given and contraception will not help the population explosion. You believe that God will make provision for the population.

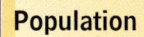

Women's Rights

You represent the right of women to have free choice and access to contraception and family-planning advice. You argue that equality for women will reduce population growth.

Population Policy

You represent a government with a successful population policy. You believe that population growth is the responsibility of individual countries. You want developing countries to take responsibility for their own population growth.

Development

You represent a group of developing countries. You believe that family planning won't help until people all over the world have a high standard of living, and equal distribution of resources.

Activity

a) Look back at Activity 1 on page 65 and fill in the table again.

b) Compare your table with the first one you made. Have you changed your mind at all? Why do you think that is?

Summary

In this unit we have looked at the causes of population growth. We have examined where growth is happening and where people live. We have also examined people's reasons for moving and why they choose to have large or small families. Finally we have looked at attempts to control population growth.

79

Sustainable Development

Source 1

An irrigation canal in northern Namibia

Namibia is a developing country in south-west Africa. Having gained its independence in 1991 it faces the challenge of trying to develop in a difficult environment. In this unit you will investigate:

- the challenges facing Namibia
- three changes people have made to improve their quality of life
- the choices facing Namibia as it develops.

- Describe the landscape in the photograph in Source 1 – what can you see?
- What evidence is there in the picture to explain how the people get water from the canal?
- Why do you think this water supply is important?

Sustainable Development

Developing Namibia

Source 2
Namibia

Large areas of farmland in Namibia are threatened by **bush encroachment**. This is where grassland is gradually taken over by bushes. It is caused by farmers overgrazing the land.

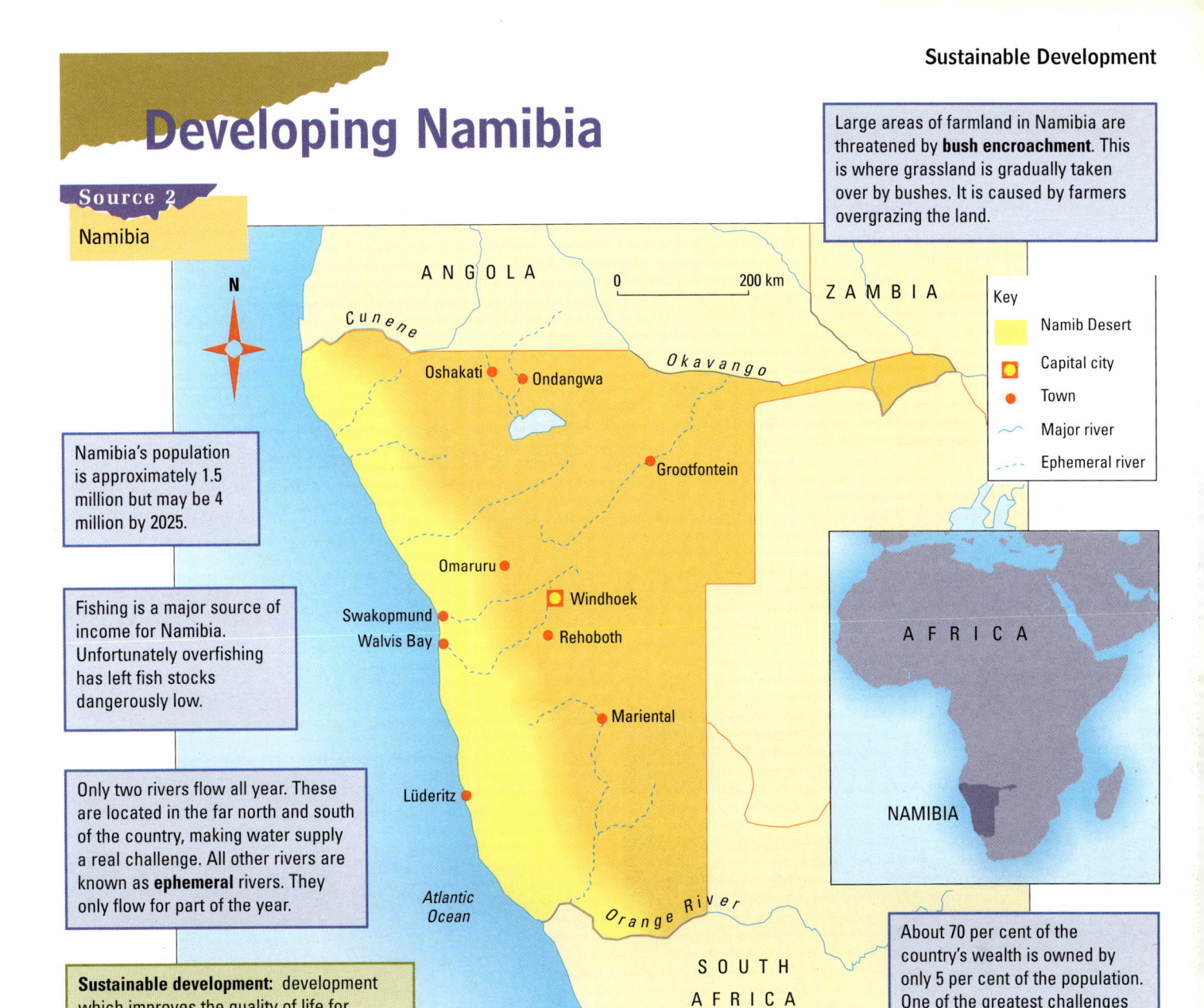

Namibia's population is approximately 1.5 million but may be 4 million by 2025.

Fishing is a major source of income for Namibia. Unfortunately overfishing has left fish stocks dangerously low.

Only two rivers flow all year. These are located in the far north and south of the country, making water supply a real challenge. All other rivers are known as **ephemeral** rivers. They only flow for part of the year.

Sustainable development: development which improves the quality of life for people today and for future generations without damaging the environment.

About 70 per cent of the country's wealth is owned by only 5 per cent of the population. One of the greatest challenges facing Namibia is to share out its wealth more equally.

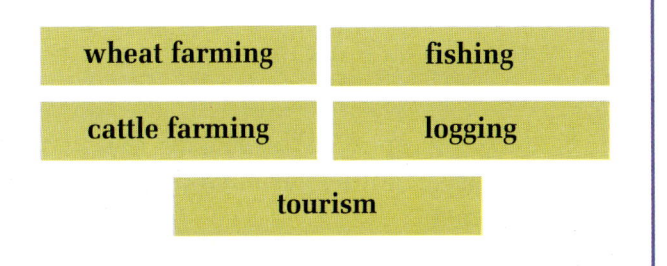

Key: Namib Desert, Capital city, Town, Major river, Ephemeral river

Towns/features on map: Angola, Zambia, Cunene, Okavango, Oshakati, Ondangwa, Grootfontein, Omaruru, Windhoek, Swakopmund, Walvis Bay, Rehoboth, Mariental, Lüderitz, Atlantic Ocean, Orange River, South Africa, Africa, Namibia

Activity

a) Look at the map in Source 2.
  i) What is the name of the desert on the western side of Namibia?
  ii) What are the names of the two rivers in Namibia that have water flowing all year?
  iii) Describe the location of these rivers.
  iv) How far is it from Windhoek to Swakopmund?
  v) Which countries border onto Namibia?
  vi) State four challenges facing Namibia.

b) Below is a list of economic activities. Choose two and explain how you would make sure they were sustainable. Use the meaning given for 'sustainable development' to help you.

- wheat farming
- fishing
- cattle farming
- logging
- tourism

81

Water in Namibia

One of the greatest challenges facing Namibia is to provide enough water for its people. The problem of low rainfall is made worse by high **evaporation**. One solution has been to create **reservoirs** to collect water during the short rainy season. The largest of these is the Hardap Dam Scheme. The dam (Source 1) was built in 1962 to supply water to the town of Mariental and to provide water for an irrigation project near the dam.

The Hardap irrigation scheme has 40 farms, each one 50 hectares in size. The farmers are metered for the water they use and pay, on average, £1,500 per year for their water. Before the dam was built, no crops could be grown in this area.

The reservoir has also created a valuable wildlife habitat. At Hardap there is now a breeding colony of pelicans as well as a popular nature trail.

As with most reservoir schemes there are some problems. High temperatures mean that 2,700 mm of water are lost each year through evaporation. Also, as rain water flows down the rivers towards the dam it carries sand with it, causing the reservoir to slowly silt up. The dam itself has also started to develop small cracks. Scientists believe this is caused by chemicals dissolved in the water from the soils in the area.

Water is mostly brought to fields through canals and irrigation channels, but circular spraying systems (see Source 2) are being gradually introduced in Namibia.

Source 1
The Hardap Dam

Source 2
Circular-spray irrigation system. This type of irrigation is expensive but very little water is wasted. Water is sprayed directly on to the crops by the huge irrigation system which slowly rotates.

Activity 1

a) Copy and complete the table on the right.

b) Overall, do you think the dam was worth building? Give both sides of the argument.

c) Is there any aspect of the scheme that may not make Hardap a fully sustainable development?

Hardap Dam Scheme	
Year dam built	
Town supplied with water	
Advantages	
Disadvantages	

Sustainable Development

One of the farmers on the scheme is Freddie Faul (Source 3). He grows mainly wheat, corn and lucerne. He employs five workers on his farm. All his produce is sold through the nearby Hardap Cooperative which has been set up by the 40 local farmers to process, pack and transport their produce.

Source 3

Freddie Faul is the chairperson of the farmers' association at the Hardap irrigation scheme. The field behind him is being irrigated with water from the reservoir.

Source 4

Part of Freddie's farm has these drainage pipes about 3 metres under the soil. From time to time Freddie completely floods his fields. This dissolves salts which have built up in the soil and washes them down through small holes in the drainage pipes.

Lucerne: a crop rather like clover, used as animal fodder. It also puts nitrogen back into the soil.

Salinisation: the gradual build up of salts in the soil, caused by high rates of evaporation in heavily irrigated areas.

Fact File . . .

Equipment on Freddie Faul's farm
- tractor
- combine harvester for corn
- baler for lucerne
- crop sprayer for pesticides
- plough
- seed drill

Activity 2

a) Using all the information on this page fill in the systems diagram below. Try to list at least three items in each box.

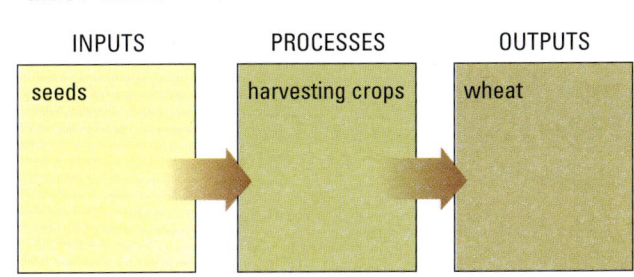

INPUTS	PROCESSES	OUTPUTS
seeds	harvesting crops	wheat

b) Look at Source 2. Can you think of one advantage and one disadvantage of the circular-spray irrigation system?

c) Look at Source 4.
   i) What problem do many farmers in hot areas who use irrigation face?
   ii) How does Freddie overcome this?

Water for Windhoek

Source 1
Diagram to show how Windhoek is supplied by water.

Windhoek is the capital city of Namibia and the largest urban area in the country. Supplying the people of Windhoek with water is a difficult task for three reasons:

- the city has a high population density in an area with low rainfall
- the population is growing fast - in the 1980s the city almost doubled in size
- people in urban areas use, on average, 8 times more water than people in rural areas

The Eastern National Water Carrier (ENWC) is a large water supply system which has the job of ensuring Windhoek has the water it needs. As you might expect it has to collect water from other parts of the country, mainly from the north, where the rainfall is higher. Source 1 shows how the ENWC supplies this water to Windhoek.

As you can see from the diagram water will eventually be drawn from the Okavango River 800km to the north on the border of Namibia. This part of the system is due to be completed by the year 2000. Some ecologists believe that this may cause problems. They say that the delicate balance of the wetlands in the north of the country may be upset.

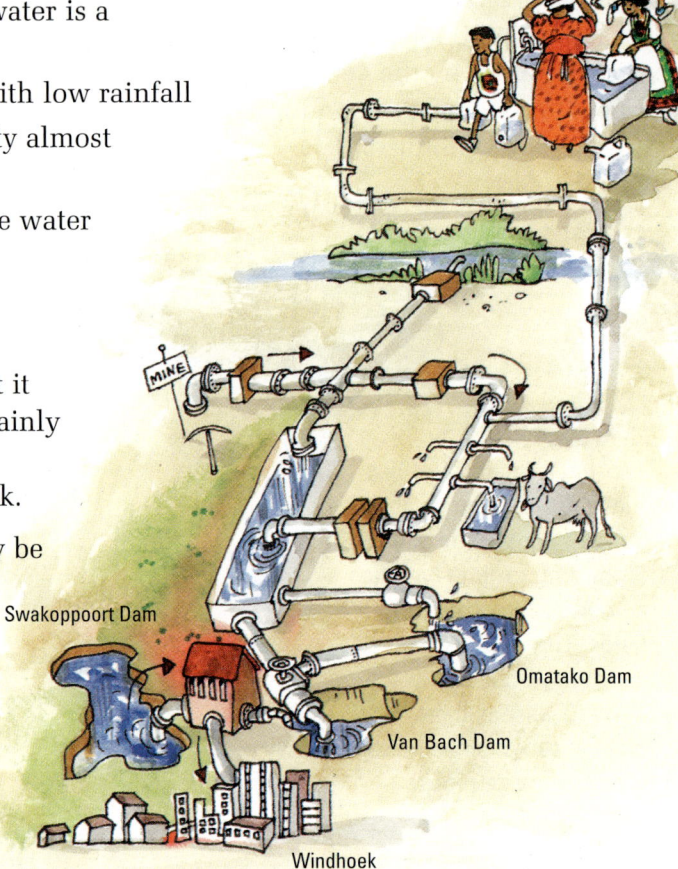

Labels on diagram: Okavango River, Swakoppoort Dam, Omatako Dam, Van Bach Dam, Windhoek

Source 2
Windhoek - a modern city which is growing fast

Activity 1

a) What does ENWC stand for?

b) Copy out these sentences, and fill in the gaps.

Windhoek has a h_____ population density in an area with l_____ rainfall. This means there is a lot of pr_____ on water supplies. Also, the population is growing f_____. In the 1980s the city almost d_____ in size. Add to that the fact that people in urban areas use, on average, _____ times more water than people in r_____ areas and the challenge of supplying w_____ is only made harder.

c) Use Source 1 to find out the names of the three reservoirs that supply water to Windhoek?

d) What is the name of the river in the north of Namibia from which water will eventually be taken for Windhoek?

Sustainable Development

Saving Water

As the population of Windhoek increases and as the city's industry becomes more developed the demand for water grows ever larger. One way to meet this growing demand is to find new sources of water. However, there is a limit to the new supplies that can be found. The Department of Water Affairs believe that it is important for people to realise the importance of conserving water to prevent future problems, especially in dry years.

A number of measures have been set up in Windhoek to reduce water consumption and these are shown in Source 3.

Source 3
How Windhoek is trying to save water

- water is being metered and the rates per cubic metre have been increased - the more water you use the more you pay
- water reclamation (recycling of water) is being established. A special purification plant has been built to recycle 12% of Windhoek's water
- education and public information campaigns have been set up like the educational game shown in Source 4

Source 4
The water game

The water saving game !!

1 WHO CAN SAVE MOST WATER? Two or more players can play this game. You need one counter each (use seeds stones and bottle tops) and a dice BEGIN →	2 YOU TURN OFF A DRIPPING TAP! Move on 2 spaces	3 YOU HAVE FILLED YOUR BATH TO THE TOP Miss a turn!	4	5 USE YOUR BATH WATER FOR THE GARDEN Have another turn
10 YOUR CISTERN LEAKS! (noisy and wasteful) Miss a turn	9	8 WASHING YOUR CAR WITH A BUCKET (not a hose pipe) Move on 3 spaces	7 YOU HAVE LEFT A HOSE PIPE RUNNING Miss 2 turns!	6
11	12 MULCH YOUR PLANTS with grass to keep the moisture in the soil Go on to No. 15	13 SHOWER rather than BATH Move on 2 spaces	14 YOUR TAP IS DRIPPING Miss a turn!	15
20 SHARE A BATH WITH A FRIEND! Throw again!	19 WASH UP IN A BOWL AND RE-USE THE WATER Move on 2 spaces	18	17	16 YOU HAVE LEFT A TAP RUNNING Go back 2 spaces!
21 PUT A BRICK INTO YOUR TOILET CISTERN Throw again!	22	23 YOU SPRAY YOUR HOUSE "to cool it off" Go back to No. 11	24	25 KEEP ON SAVING WATER!

1 Play the Namibian water saving game

2 Why do you think the Namibian government want school children to play this game?

Activity 2

a) Water is pumped along the pipes. What moves the water along the canal?

b) Why doesn't water drain out of the canal?

c) Write about the three ways the government is trying to save water in Windhoek (Source 3).

d) Imagine you have been given the job of designing a board game to help Namibian children aged eleven learn about ways water can be saved in the home.

　i) Make a list of 10 ideas for water saving (eg. use your bath water to water the garden)

　ii) design your game to include your ten points

　iii) try playing your game

85

Fishing for success

In recent years Namibia has seen a massive growth in its fishing industry, making use of some of the richest fishing areas in the world. The main fish caught are pilchards, anchovies, mackerel and hake. Source 1 shows the weight of the pilchard catch each year.

Before Namibia's **independence** much of the fishing off the coastline was by foreign ships and very little profit came into the country. Not only that, but overfishing was causing the fish stocks to get very low.

In 1991 the Namibian Government decided to act and decided to do these things:

- to set **quotas** on the amount of fish that could be caught to allow the stocks to build up
- to limit the number of foreign ships fishing in Namibian waters by giving Namibians most of the licences to fish
- to encourage more fish processing to take place in Namibia, providing jobs within the country.

Source 2

This boat is fishing for hake from the port of Walvis Bay. It usually spends three or four days at sea before returning to unload.

Source 3

These women are filleting the fish before it is packed and sent to markets in Europe.

Source 1

Pilchard catches in Namibia, 1950–95

Year	Thousands of tonnes
1950	143
1955	257
1960	229
1965	657
1970	1057
1975	571
1980	36
1985	56
1990	92
1995	91

The government's plan has been very successful. The number of Namibian ships has doubled in five years and the contribution to the economy has more than trebled. By the year 2000, fishing is expected to represent 25 per cent of the national economy compared with less than 3 per cent in 1990.

Sustainable Development

Northern Fisheries is one company that was set up in 1992 as a result of the government's policies. Based in Walvis Bay, they fish entirely for hake (Source 2). The company started with just six employees and now has almost 300 people working for them on their boats or in the processing factory (Source 3); 75 per cent of their fresh fish is now flown direct to Europe (Source 4).

Central to Namibia's success has been the policy not to allow overfishing. If the fishing industry is to remain sustainable then strict enforcement of the quotas is essential. To ensure this every ship has an inspector on board who carefully checks and records fish catches. Special high-speed boats also carry out patrols in Namibian waters.

The future for Namibian fishing looks very promising and it is estimated that by the year 2000 the country could be earning £300 million a year.

Source 4

Fresh hake from Namibia is air freighted to Europe

Activity 1

a) Sort the list below under the correct headings on the table:

fish trimmed	bones removed
electricity	fish for home market
polystyrene (for boxes)	fish packed
remove bones	
freezing	
fish roe	
boxes made	
ammonia (for freezing process)	
sorting fish (for quality)	
fish meal (made from head, tail, etc.)	

Inputs	Processes	Outputs
hake caught at sea	fish cleaned	fish for export

b) Copy and complete the table below:

Action taken by government	Why it was done	Evidence of success (quote fact)
1.		
2.		
3.		

c) i) Using Source 1 plot a line graph to show the pilchard catch from 1950 to 1995.

ii) Use the statements listed below to explain the changes in the line graph you have drawn and label them on your graph in suitable places:

- quotas on fish catches introduced
- sharp rise in catches
- quotas gradually increased as stocks recover
- period of overfishing
- fish stocks fall fast due to overfishing

Small-scale sustainable development

Natalie lives in the village of Ogongo with her eight year old son Erasmus. Ogongo is in northern Namibia, near Oshakati, which is one of the poorest parts of the country. Natalie works on a market-garden project. This is a small-scale development scheme that was set up by a Namibian aid agency. Timo has been sent by the agency to talk to Natalie about her work (Source 1).

Timo: When did you start work on your market garden?

Natalie: June 1994. There are six of us. We're all women and have one hectare of land each.

Timo: How did you learn about growing vegetables?

Natalie: In workshops. There were different ones on planting seeds, using chemicals, irrigation and marketing. Now we train local women.

Timo: How do you do that?

Natalie: We train two women each. There are six hectares of land for them to use on the project. The idea is that they go back to their villages and teach what they have learnt to others. In that way our ideas can be spread to as many people as possible.

Timo: How much help do you get from aid agencies?

Natalie: A lot. Especially at first. They put in irrigation pipes (Source 2) and bought us pumps, fencing, seeds, fertilisers and pesticides. We're also each paid N$300 (£50) a month. But all money will stop at the end of next year.

Timo: What happens then?

Natalie: We're on our own! But we're saving all the money we earn in the bank. I'm looking forward to the project sustaining itself. We'll still get advice if we need it.

Timo: Could I buy some of your carrots?

Natalie: Have some free. We've a lot of carrots this month. Last week we took 200 kg to market and sold them for N$2 (40p) a kilo.

Timo: Thanks. They look delicious.

Source 1

Timo gives Natalie advice on how to water her carrots.

Source 2

Irrigation pipes are used to water the fields. Can you see the water dripping out?

Sustainable Development

Source 3

A plan of the market-garden project.

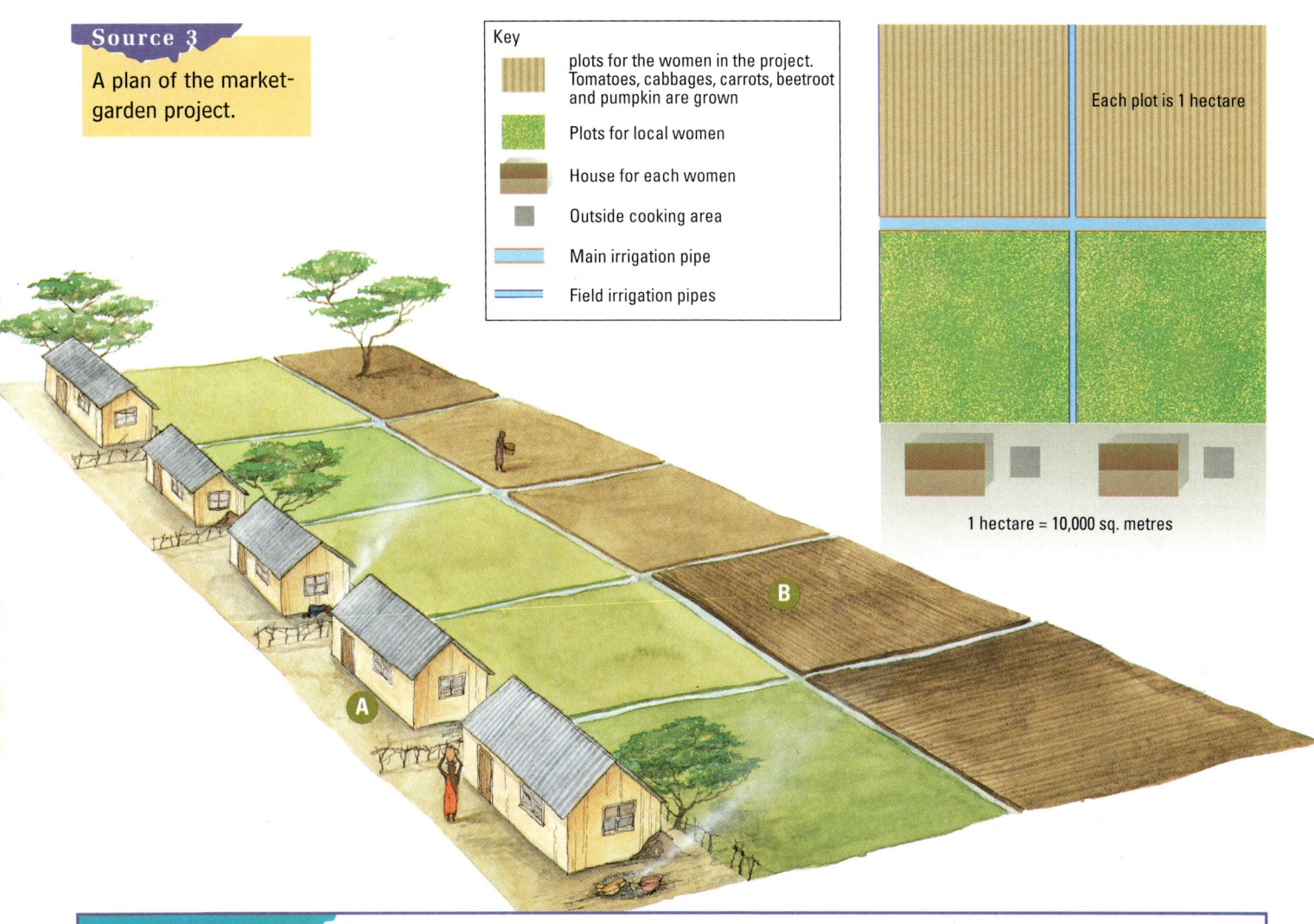

Key
- plots for the women in the project. Tomatoes, cabbages, carrots, beetroot and pumpkin are grown
- Plots for local women
- House for each women
- Outside cooking area
- Main irrigation pipe
- Field irrigation pipes

Each plot is 1 hectare

1 hectare = 10,000 sq. metres

Activity

a) Copy out the sentences that are true:
- The north is the richest part of Namibia.
- Natalie learnt about growing vegetables in workshops.
- The vegetables are watered by spray irrigation.
- Twelve local women are trained on the project.

b) Look at Source 3. Write out the sentences below in the correct order:
- Water is sprayed on to the crops.
- Small pipes take water to each field.
- Water is pumped from the canal.
- The main pipe carries water through the project.

c) Natalie lives in house A. How far is it to her field of carrots at B?

d) Explain how the Ogongo project helps more than the six women who live there.

e) Timo goes back to visit Natalie a year later. Write down at least five questions he could ask her. Timo is interested to find out if the project is sustainable.

The green plan

You have studied three development projects in Namibia. The government wants to make sure that all future development in the country is sustainable. They have written a document called 'The Green Plan' (Source 1). This contains guidelines on **sustainable development** for government ministries and private companies. It encourages them to work together to 'secure for present and future generations a safe and healthy environment and a prosperous economy'.

To write the Green Plan, government ministers met to discuss their ideas. Read what each minister is saying in Source 2 – but be careful! Not all of the ministers are in favour of sustainable development.

Source 1
The Green Plan

NAMIBIA'S GREEN PLAN
(Environment and Development)

Namibia's Green Plan to secure for present and future generations a safe and healthy environment and a prosperous economy

REPUBLIC OF NAMIBIA

Source 2
Government ministers discuss the Green Plan

Minister of Mines & Energy

A third of Namibia's wealth and 76 per cent of our exports come from mining. We have uranium, diamonds, copper and other metals. Mining must come first. The environment second.

Minister of Fisheries & Marine Resources

Investment in the fishing industry must be a priority. We should help companies expand and export as much fish as they can. This will bring money into Namibia.

The President

Land, water, air, plants and animals are the wealth of Namibia. We can have food, shelter and money from these resources if we manage them wisely. It is a challenge, but by working together we can achieve sustainable development.

Sustainable Development

Activity

a) What is the aim of the Green Plan?

b) Name the two ministers who are not in favour of sustainable development.

c) The ministers in question b) lose their jobs. Write down what you think the new ministers might say. They are in favour of sustainable development.

d) Imagine you work for the Ministry of Agriculture, Water and Rural Development. You have been asked to produce a poster showing tourists in Namibia how they could conserve water. Make sure your poster is eye-catching and informative. Can you improve on the poster in Source 3?

Source 3
A Namibian government poster:

SELL SOME CATTLE 2

USE IT WISELY 1

PLANT MORE TREES 3

3 WAYS TO SAVE WATER

the Department of Water Affairs, Namibia, in collaboration with UNICEF

Minister of Agriculture, Water & Rural Development: We must give everyone safe and reliable water and teach them how to conserve it. Soil erosion and deforestation must also be controlled.

Minister of Wildlife, Conservation & Tourism: Namibia's wildlife attracts tourists and provides jobs to local people. We can use our lions, elephants, wildebeest, giraffes and zebras to teach tourists about conservation.

Minister of Health & Social Services: We must control population growth. Today Namibia is sparsely populated, but we are growing at 3 per cent a year. This growth will make it difficult to achieve sustainable development. We'll not have enough schools, hospitals, jobs or land.

Summary

In this unit you have learnt what sustainable development is. You have investigated three case studies of sustainable development from Namibia. You have learnt that both large- and small-scale projects can be sustainable and that it is important for the people and the government of a country to work together and share their ideas. As we reach the twenty-first century, achieving sustainable development is one of the major challenges facing our planet.

Issues in geography

Our world is one where there is a lot of **change**. As the world continues changing and developing geographers investigate some of the issues which **challenge** people and places in the world today. In this book you have learnt about some of these issues. You have found out that people have different views and make different **choices** about an issue. For example the choices people make about supplying water to Namibia's capital city Windhoek will be very different from the choices people make about supplying water to London. It is very important when you make decisions for the future that you think about the places and all the people involved.

volcanic eruption

urban growth

agricultural change

nuclear power

coastal erosion

Sustainable Development

deforestation

air pollution

flooding

Activity

Choose **three** issues on the island that you know about. Some possible issues are labelled. For each one answer the questions below. Your answers should be as detailed as possible. Remember to include information about real places you have studied.

1. Explain what the issue might be at this place.
2. Where have you studied this issue?
3. Why is there an issue here?
4. What do different groups of people think about the issue?
5. What do you think should happen in the future?

Glossary

Abrasion Process of river erosion in which boulders are used to break off pieces of rock in the river.

Abrasion When the waves pick up sand, pebbles and boulders and crash them against the base of a cliff, eroding it.

Agribusiness Large farms, often owned by companies which aim to make as much money as they can, being run as businesses.

Attrition When blocks of rocks, eroded from cliffs, are crashed against each other and are broken into smaller pieces eventually becoming sand.

Backwash The water draining back down the beach after a wave has broken.

Beach An area of sand or shingle found between the coastline and the shoreline.

Birth rate The number of births per thousand people in any year.

Broads Lakes in the Norfolk Broads.

Bush encroachment Where grassland is gradually taken over by bushes.

Carnivore Meat eating animals e.g. hunting animals such as lions.

Channel Between the river banks where the river water flows.

Choropleth map A map that uses different shading to show information.

Coastline The line along the land reached by the highest tides.

Competitive plant community Plants have to fight with other plants for light, water and nutrients to gain what they need to grow.

Condensation Water vapour in the air becomes water droplets after cooling.

Conservation When people try to use resources (e.g. farmland) carefully and protect the environment.

Constructive waves Short, separate waves where the swash and backwash move up and down the beach before the next wave breaks. These waves tend to build the beach up.

Consumer Animals which gain their food eating plants and other animals.

Contraception Different methods of birth control.

Culling When people kill animals to control their numbers.

Death rate The number of deaths per thousand people in any year.

Decay Leaves rot on the forest floor.

Decomposition Plant material is broken down to release the nutrients.

Deposition Builds up new landforms from eroded and transported material which is put down somewhere new.

Destructive waves Tall, more frequent waves where the breaking wave plunges onto the beach churning up the beach material so that the backwash can carry it back down the beach. These waves tend to erode the beach.

Dominant The tallest and most important plant in a community.

Dot distribution map A map that uses dots to show where a certain number of things are.

Drainage basin Area of land within which water flows into the river and its tributaries.

Ecosystem Living community of plants and animals related to the physical environment in which they are growing.

Emigration Moving out of an area.

Erosion Is when rivers, moving ice, waves or winds pick up the broken rocks made by weathering, move them and use them to wear away the land.

Evaporation Water on the earth's surface is heated up and becomes water vapour in the air.

Family planning schemes Using birth control (contraception) to plan the number of children in a family.

Fetch The distance over which waves can travel towards a coastline.

Floodplain Flat land next to the river.

Food chain The energy from plants is passed along a chain of living things.

Forced migration When a migrant doesn't have a choice about moving.

Groundwater flow Water underground moving sideways through the rock.

Habitat Natural home of plants and animals.

Herbivore Animals which feed off plants e.g. grass eating animals such as cows and zebra.

Hydraulic action When the force of the waves squashes air into cracks in cliffs, loosening rocks which eventually fall into the sea.

Immigration Moving into an area.

Impermeable rock Rock which will not allow water to pass through it.

Interlocking spurs Areas of slightly higher land on the sides of a river in the hills between which the river is forced to bend.

Lateral erosion Land worn away at the sides of a river.

Levée High banks along the sides of a river (usually in the lowlands).

Longshore drift When material is moved along a coastline by waves which break onto the beach at an angle.

Lucerne A crop rather like clover which is used as animal fodder. It also puts nitrogen back in the soil.

Manufactured resources Products that have been through a manufacturing process to turn them into something that people want.

Meander Larger bend in a river (in the lowlands).

Migration Moving in or out of an area.

Mouth Place where the river water meets the sea.

National Parks Areas of land set aside by the government, for conservation, recreation and leisure, managed by a Planning Board.

Natural increase When the birth rate is higher than the death rate, causing a rise in the total population.

Natural resources Materials which the earth provides, e.g. coal, oil, food etc.

Nutrients Food sources for plants.

Omnivore Animals which eat both plants and meat.

Overfishing When so many fish are caught that the fish population cannot recover naturally, causing the number of fish to decline.

Ox-bow lake Semi-circular lake on the floodplain.

Pastoral farming The raising of animals such as beef or dairy cattle, sheep, pigs and poultry.

Percolation Water seeping downwards into the ground.

Plunge pool Deep water below the waterfall.

Porous rock A rock with holes in it through which ground water can pass and in which groundwater can be stored.

Population The number of people in an area.

Population density The number of people per area of land, i.e. how crowded somewhere is.

Population explosion The rapid increase in world population.

Population pyramids A diagram that shows us how many males and females there are in a country at different age groups.

Precipitation Water from the atmosphere such as rain and snow.

Producer Plants which provide the food for animals.

Push-pull factors Name given to the reasons why people are drawn to move to an area usually a city (**urban pull**), and want to move away from somewhere else, (**rural push**). This describes the phenomena of population shift from rural areas to urban ones.

Quota Limit places on an activity, e.g. the number of fish allowed to be caught.

Recycling Used more than once.

Reservoir An artificial lake created by the building of a dam.

Rural depopulation When people move away from rural (countryside) areas to go to the cities.

Savanna Vegetation found in some tropical areas which is a mixture of grasses and trees.

Set-aside payments Payments made to farmers by the European Union if they leave some of their land unused, in order to reduce farm outputs.

Shore The strip of land between the coastline and the low-tide level.

Silt Fine material deposited by a river (usually making very fertile soil).

Source Point where the river begins.

Spit An area of sand or shingle deposited by longshore drift, which either extends at a gentle angle out to sea or grows across a river estuary.

Storm surge High waves blowing across the sea, caused by very strong winds (caused by low air pressure).

Surface run-off Water which flows overland in rivers and streams.

Sustainable development Development which improves peoples' lives without damaging the environment for future generations.

Swash The water thrown up the beach by a breaking wave.

Transpiration Water loss into the atmosphere from vegetation on the earth's surface.

Transport Is when the agent of erosion (rivers, moving ice, waves or wind) moves the rocks broken down by weathering, from one place to another.

Tributary A small river which supplies water to a large river.

Trophic level Food level.

Tundra Inuit (Eskimo) word for the vast treeless plains found mainly inside the Arctic Circle.

Vertical erosion Land worn away by the river cutting downwards.

Water cycle Rain water which comes from the atmosphere is returned to the atmosphere by evaporation as part of a continuous process of recycling.

Waterfall Fast flowing water down a steep slope.

Weathering Is when rocks are broken down by the effects of the weather, plants or animals.

Index

Africa
    development 80–91
    savanna 36, 47, 48–9
agribusiness 53
agriculture see farming
Alpine environment 56
Antarctica 6
Arctic 60–1

Bangladesh 31, 72
beach 23, 26, 27, 28
birth rate 66
Brazil
    farming 42
    rivers 5
bush encroachment 81

China, one child policy 76
choropleth map 67, 69
cliffs 23, 24–5, 26
climate 40–1, 43, 44–5
coastline 21, 22, 29
coasts 20–35
    landforms 24–5, 28–9, 32
    processes 22–31
    protection 30
conservation, ecosystems 48–9, 53
countryside 51, 52–3

dam 16–17, 82
death rate 66
deposition 9, 10, 26, 28
desert 81
desertification 63
developed countries 59, 75
developing countries see less developed countries
development
    coast 34–5
    sustainable 80–93
development plan 88–9
development projects 82–7
distribution map 68, 69
drought, adaptation 45

ecosystems 36–49
    savanna 36, 41, 44–9
Egypt
    farming 43
    floods 17
environments, management 50–63
erosion
    coastal 20, 24–5, 26, 30
    river 8–9, 10
Europe, population density 69

family planning schemes 72, 73, 76–7
farming 42–3, 56
    Mediterranean 63
    Namibia 82–3, 86–7
    UK 52–3

fishing 84–5
floodplain 10–11
floods 4, 12–19, 21
    prevention 16–17
food chain 46
food resources 42, 74–5
France, national park 56–7
fresh water 6–7

game, rivers 18–19
graphs 66, 73, 84

habitat, wildlife 37
hazards, coast 30–1

India, population 73
irrigation 80, 82–3, 86

Japan, population 64

land use 47, 52–3, 63
landforms see coasts; rivers
leisure activities 54–5
less developed countries 58, 59, 75, 80–91
longshore drift 26–7, 28–9

maps, OS 9, 11, 28, 29, 32–3
market gardening 86–7
Mediterranean landscapes 62–3
migration 66, 70–1
Mississippi, River 14–15

Namibia, development 80–91
national parks 51, 56–7
Nile, River 17
nutrients, plants 38–9

oil pipeline 60–1
Okavango, River 90
one child policy 76
overgrazing 81

Peru, population 70–1
pollution 55
    oil 60–1
    water 59
population 64–79
    change 66–7, 76–7
    density 68
    growth 65–7, 72
    pressure 78–9
    pyramids 73
precipitation 6, 12
push-pull factors 70–1

rainfall 11–12, 15, 38, 40–1
rainforest 39, 41
reservoir 16, 82
resources 74–5

rivers 4–19
    channel 8, 12, 16
    management 16
    processes 8–9, 10–11
    valleys in lowlands 10–11
    valleys in uplands 8–9
rural depopulation 56
rural landscape 52–3
Russia, oil pollution 61

savanna ecosystem 44–9
small-scale development 86–7
soil erosion 63
spits 28–9
surface runoff 6, 12–13
sustainable development 80–93

Tees, River 8–9, 11, 16
temperate environment 40
Thailand, population 76–7
Thames Barrier 31
tourism 63
transport 26–7
tropical environment 41
tundra 60

UK
    Dorset coast 27, 32–3, 35
    East Anglia 28–9, 52
    farming 43, 52–3
    national parks 51
    Norfolk Broads 54–5
    population 68, 71, 73
    water supply 58
USA
    Alaska 60
    floods 14–15

valleys 8–9, 10–11
vegetation 36, 40, 41, 44–5

water
    management 58–9
    pollution 59
    supply 5, 58, 80, 90–1
water cycle 6–7
waterfall 8, 9
waterways 54–5
waves 22–3, 26
weathering 26
wildlife 46–7